"*Divine Grace: The Power That Illuminates Your Soul* tells the story of one woman's profound spiritual journey. The author is a wisdom gatherer and through this marvelous book, Fredericka shares truths and insights that will inspire every reader. I found this book to be absolutely wonderful."

—Caroline Myss, five-time NY Times bestselling author of
ANATOMY of the SPIRIT and *DEFY GRAVITY*

≈

"This extraordinary book is a journey into the nature of the spiritual experience. I highly recommend this engaging, empowering and insightful book to anyone who longs to discover the essence of their soul. *Divine Grace: The Power That Illuminates Your Soul* is a generous gift to us all."

—Michelle Cromer, author of *Exit Strategy; Thinking Outside the Box*

≈

"Many books have been written about the awakening of the heart to the presence of the Sacred Heart. What sets *Divine Grace: The Power That Illuminates Your Soul* apart is that it is not only about the awakening but also about staying awake."

—Jim Curtan, Spiritual Director and Archetypal Consultant

≈

"Fredericka Close is someone who writes from the depths of her personal experience. There is no substitute for such sincerity. Her insights about grace are truly a gift from Spirit. Grace flows down like water until it reaches our soul and dispels our fear.
Thank you Ms. Close for your clarity and sharing."

—Virginia Nemetz, Ph.D., author of *Stone Child's Mother: A Jungian Narrative Reflection on the Mother Archetype* and a book of poems: *Swans I Have Known*

≈

"A wise guide through the rocky and confounding journey of the soul. Along the way it teaches a powerful skill called discernment which gives us access to the healing wisdom of our hearts."

—Ellen Gunter, author of *Earth Calling* and Spiritual Director

DIVINE GRACE

Divine Grace:
The Power That Illuminates Your Soul

Fredericka Close,
R.N., A.C.R.N.

HISPUBLISHING GROUP

www.hispubg.com
A division of HISpecialists, llc

Inquiries should be addressed to Fredericka Close
c/o HIS Publishing Group, PO Box 12516, Dallas, Texas 75225.

Published by HIS Publishing Group,
a Division of Human Improvement Specialists, llc
Contact: info@hispubg.com

Cover by Lindsey Look
Edited by Lorraine Alexson
Design by Anton Khodakovsky

Library of Congress Control Number: 2013907138

Printed and bound in the United States of America

1 2 3 4 5 6 7 8 9 10

Close, Fredericka
Divine grace: the power that illuminates your soul /
Fredericka Close; foreword by Jim Curtan

Includes bibliography and index.
1. Spiritual life. 2. Mysticism. 3. Inspirational. I. Title

ISBN 13-978-0-615-77798-6 (soft cover)
ISBN 13-978-0-615-77799-3 (hard cover)

Permissions acknowledgments appear on page 269–270

For Caroline Myss,

the amazing spiritual teacher who set off a depth charge in my soul that will reverberate for all eternity.

Namaste, with great love.

TABLE OF CONTENTS

FOREWORD

by Jim Curtan

FREDDIE CLOSE DEDICATES THIS BOOK to our mutual friend and teacher, Caroline Myss. It's through our connection to Caroline that Freddie and I became acquainted. In 1997, two days after I had been diagnosed with cancer, I came across Caroline's book, *Why People Don't Heal and How They Can*. I thought, "I could really use this information," so I bought the book and read it immediately. Several months later I became one of Caroline's students, and a couple of years after that, Caroline generously invited me to teach with her. Over the years I became increasingly aware of one of the workshop participants, a woman with an uncommonly still and steady presence. She approached me one day and told me she prayed for me every day. I assumed she was praying for my continued healing from cancer, and I thanked her. She told me her praying for me had nothing to do with the cancer; she just prayed for me. I was speechless—an uncommon occurrence. The woman is Freddie Close, the author of this book.

There are people who spent their lives in prayer and contemplation. It was traditionally thought that, in order to dedicate their lives to such rigorous and selfless practice, it was necessary for these people to withdraw from the world. When I was growing up, my mother would send prayer requests along with offerings to cloistered nuns, nuns who live hidden lives of prayerful presence. Today, many of these prayerful presences live among us; Caroline Myss calls them "mystics without monasteries." Freddie is surely one of these.

I've often reflected on the gospel passage in which Jesus' disciples ask Him to "teach us to pray." In doing so, whether they realize it or not, the disciples are asking Jesus to reveal intimate details about His deepest, most personal and private relationship with the Divine—the treasure in His heart. I wonder whether He paused (I would have) to ask God whether He had to give even that away.

While Freddie is sparing in the extent to which she shares the external events of her life, offering only what is essential to our understanding how they are related to the awakening and developing of her inner life, she is fearless and generous in revealing this most intimate part of her, the awakening of her heart to Divine Spirit, and with it, the commitment to be a prayerful presence in the world.

Many books have been written about the awakening of the heart to the presence of the Sacred Heart. What sets *Divine Grace: The Power That Illuminates Your Soul* apart is that it is not only about the awakening but also about staying awake.

Jesus' last words to his disciples as he is being arrested and taken away are, "Couldn't you stay awake with me one hour?" Throughout the book, Freddie generously offers her "spiritual exercises" for staying awake and continuing to awaken still more.

(It is a myth that we experience only one spiritual awakening.)

The late Jesuit priest and master storyteller Anthony de Mello said that if you had to take all of the great wisdom traditions of the world, Buddhism, Christian, Hindu, Islam, Judaism, and all of the others – and reduce them all to two words, those two words would be "Wake up."

Throughout this book, Freddie frequently refers to the great Spanish mystic, John of the Cross, who famously said that God always initiates the Encounter. God issues the invitation. Our choice is whether to accept or decline the invitation.

Over and over throughout this lovely book, Freddie, encourages us to accept it.

—Jim Curtan

The Ritual of Smudging with Sage

Every morning before meditation I perform the Native American ritual of smudging with sage.

Steps of Ritual

❋ I begin by placing a seashell with burning sage on an altar near where I meditate. I cup the rising smoke in my hands and bring it over the top of my head while saying the following words: "Thank you for clearing my mind so good and pure thoughts come into it." I move my hands to my throat area, again cupping the rising smoke from the seashell and say: "Thank you for clearing my throat so my words and actions are good and pure." I move to my heart, cupping the rising smoke, and say: "Thank you for opening my heart to the blessings of this day and all the blessings that are on their way to me." I move on in a single gesture to my body, cupping the rising smoke in my hands, and, bringing my hands over the top of my head and down along my body to my leg area, I say: "Thank you for this body temple, this vehicle that allows me to experience You and for its health, strength, stamina, and beauty."

❁ I then honor the four cardinal directions while holding the seashell in one hand under the burning sage in my other hand. I face the east and acknowledge the Spirits of the east: "This is the place of new beginnings, inspiration, and illumination. Thank you for this new day and all the opportunities to see You and experience You in the details of this day and all the days of my life. Thank you for calling me to be in Spirit so I may be open to receive Your inspiration. Thank you for illuminating my light and my shadow and my path of compassion, unconditional love, forgiveness, and reverence for all of life. I am so truly appreciative, thankful, and blessed."

❁ I turn to face north. I acknowledge the Spirits of the north: "This is the place of words and knowledge and wisdom. Thank you for a deeper understanding of the power of words and the guidance to choose them wisely with compassion, unconditional love, forgiveness, and reverence for all life. Thank you for the knowledge that comes my way, the beings that carry it, seen and unseen, and the wisdom that knowledge reveals within my being. I am so truly appreciative, thankful, and blessed."

❁ I turn to face west. I acknowledge the Spirits of the west: "This is the place of courage, the going within place. Thank you for the courage to embrace my light and my shadow and my path of compassion, unconditional love, forgiveness, and reverence for all life. Thank you for Your still, small voice, which calls me within to Your presence, the place of peace that is beyond human understanding. I am so truly appreciative, thankful, and blessed."

❋ I turn to face south. I acknowledge the Spirits of the south: "This is the place of innocence, trust, faith, joy, and belief. Thank you for letting me know You are my constant companion and comforter, closer than my very breath, and for the knowing that I have nothing to fear, for You are my Beloved. I am so truly appreciative, thankful, and blessed."

≈

This ritual will be helpful to you on your soul's journey of illumination. It will help you to remove the barriers to love and to love unconditionally until you and the Beloved are One.

PRELUDE

The Morning of Inspiration

O N THE MORNING OF MARCH 5, 2009, I awoke and could not go back to sleep. I got up looking forward to a precious "no-time-constraint" meditation. It was about four in the morning so I knew I had plenty of time to indulge myself before work. I had no way of knowing I was to be given a most profound gift that morning. As always, I began my morning ritual with the Native American tradition of "smudging" with the herb sage, followed by a meditation. For those of you who are unfamiliar with the tradition of smudging, let me briefly explain my understanding of the ritual. Sage is lighted, and the smoke of the sage is used to cleanse or purify the person performing the ritual. Think of it as similar to the use of water in purifying rituals in almost all religious and spiritual traditions: Buddhist, Christian, Jewish, Muslim, and Shinto, to name a few.

I held a leaf of burning sage over a beautiful seashell that I had found on a beach. As I was honoring the Spirits of the west, my focus was drawn to an unusual sight in front of my eyes.

The smoke from the sage was flowing down through the sage leaf into the seashell instead of rising above, as it usually does. The shell filled completely with smoke, and then the smoke, ever so gracefully, flowed over the edge of the shell like a mysterious waterfall. This visual experience of the smoke cascading over the brim of the seashell was most comforting. I had a sense that all was well, a sensation similar to that of sitting by a still pond. The phrase "Be still and know that I am God" came to mind and filled me with peace (Psalm 46:10, Old Testament).

Then that visual image of smoke pouring over the rim of the seashell like a waterfall ignited a knowing within me that Divine grace was flowing down through the top of my head and on through my power centers, or chakras (*chakra* is a Sanskrit term meaning "wheel" or "disc"), and out into the space around me. That water was a metaphor for the powerful flow of Divine grace. I was filled with bliss and awe, and I was unaware of my surroundings. All this must have happened in an instant. It left me breathless.

Right after the experience, an awareness struck me that was hard to take in. I knew that I was to write about the experience I had just had. Immediately after, self-doubt and a sense of not being "good enough" came flooding into my mind. As I was gathering my writing materials at 5:24 that morning, the world of ego and self-recrimination began a dialogue in my head. "Who are you to write anything, let alone on the subject of Divine grace that only mystics, theologians, scholars, poets, and other great authors have written about so eloquently and extensively?" Yet the experience I had had was a precious gift, resonating profoundly within my soul. I knew that avoiding writing about it was not an option. I collected as much courage and composure as I could muster and began to write.

The words that came to me that morning are my humble attempt to describe the ineffable experience I had. Since the words necessarily come through my limited ability to convey a magnificent experience, they certainly cannot do justice to the exquisiteness of the gift. Yet I feel strongly that my words are the best ones I can offer. I hesitate to change them as they transferred my experience to a physical dimension, manifested on paper. The words felt as though they were flowing through me rather than my having thought about what I should write. I offer this writing with great humility and love.

THE WATERFALL OF DIVINE GRACE

The flow of Divine grace enters our crown chakra and fills it with pure clear water, if you will. Think of the mountain springs in the Himalayas, fresh from snowmelt, purifying our awareness and consciousness of the Oneness of creation.

This amazing water overflows to purify our third eye chakra, and we understand that it is washing away clouds of judgment and duality, allowing precious moments of clear vision. Saint Teresa of Avila, a sixteenth-century mystic, describes it as "seeing God in the details" of life from and with a mystical vision or perception.

Divine grace directs this pure stream of water to flow into our throat chakra and begins to clear away the constrictions of our narrow will and perspective. We begin to become aware of an energy that is building pressure behind the resistance of our beliefs and egotistical ways of trying to control our world according to our standards.

The pressure now is too strong; it breaks through and begins to flow into our broken hearts. The cleansing waters of Divine grace fill the chambers of our hearts, wherein reside hurt,

3

abandonment, mistrust, restriction, resentment, and inability to forgive ourselves and others. As the chambers are filled with the living waters of unconditional love, we begin to expand our awareness, our ability to forgive and the beginning of unconditional love starts to trickle in.

The Divine grace that guides the flow of this water is now trickling into our solar plexus chakra, which holds our self-esteem and intuition. We are opening and trusting that the cleansing waters of Divine grace are washing away long-held beliefs of separation from our Creator. Our consciousness is becoming open to knowing that we can navigate the flow of our life from a higher and gentler way of being in the earthly experience. Guidance is trickling through, and the cleansing waters of Divine grace are clearing away our resistance.

The survival fears of our sacral chakra are being soothed by the unstoppable love of Divine grace as it washes over our sense of being alone in this, our worldly experience. We are awakening to the power of the current that is moving debris, boulders, this rubble of the broken dreams and disappointments of our constricted past.

The current of the cleansing force is now a powerful waterfall. It crashes down on the things that impede its flow and has its way with our doubts, judgments, and constrictions of our root chakra. It breaks through the barrier of our limited sense of self. It overflows the banks of our limited vision of life and floods our experience of life with the stunning mystical experience of living life as it was intended!

≈

It took some time to shift my awareness back to the time constraints of my busy life schedule, and I reluctantly began to get on with the seemingly mundane tasks of eating breakfast and preparing to go to work. I was periodically overwhelmed with a sense of awe and struggled most of the day to connect with the responsibilities of my job. As I write this today, I wonder why I had never thought to take that day off to bask in the bliss of this most wondrous experience. Each time I reflect on the gift I received, I am filled with gratitude and humility and can still "touch" a sense of the awe of that morning.

Two days before this experience I had received an email from a website I had never been in touch with before. To this day I do not know how I appeared on that website's email list. I chuckle as I reflect on that last sentence; could it have been a coincidence? You know what they say about coincidences, there are no such things. Anyway, that email was an invitation to attend a free webinar about becoming a spiritual author. I registered for the event since for some time I had been playing with the idea of writing a book and thought that since the event was free, I had nothing to lose. The webinar took place on the same evening of my experience. Another coincidence? Who knows, but it certainly was an interesting sequence of events.

About two and a half years after the morning when I received this inspiration, I was reading an article and came across this sentence: "Deep calls to deep in the roar of your waterfalls." It was from a particular translation of Psalm 42:7. I immediately looked up the quotation and was confused by what I found. This section of the psalm contains the word *cataracts* instead of *waterfall.* On further exploration, I learned that the word *cataract,* what we think of today as an opaqueness of the lens of our eyes, is a secondary definition of *cataract.* The primary definition is "a high or large waterfall." It comes from the Greek word *katarakt,* meaning waterfall. Here is more of the psalm: "Deep calls to deep in the roar of your cataracts; all your breakers and billows have passed over me. By day the Lord bestows his grace, and by night I have his song, a prayer to my living God." I was taken aback by the power of that prayer and had a deeper appreciation for the metaphor of the waterfall that I was given for Divine grace.

I humbly offer this book to you in the hope that something contained in it will ignite and fuel a yearning for wholeness within that you may have been sensing. For those of you who have already begun your soul's journey, I hope there will be something of value within these pages to assist you on your way to wholeness.

This soul journey is the call to align ourselves with the Truth of who we truly are and that Divine grace is the power that will illuminate the path of our soul's journey to wholeness. When I refer to the Truth of who we are, I mean the Source of our being, the Creator of the universe.

INTRODUCTION

I HAVE BEEN ON A SPIRITUAL PATH for more than five decades. As is true with many journeys, I found twists and turns rather than a straight road and was unaware of the stunning revelations ahead. As previously described, I received a spiritual instruction to write this book. What I have produced is, rather than a book, a journal of my experience of illumination. The journey of writing has changed my life in dramatic and entirely unexpected ways.

My journey has brought me to a place in my soul that I have read about for many years in the ancient writings of the masters and the spiritual teachers of our times who tell the story of a mystical path to wholeness in understandable language. However, reading about the path to wholeness and experiencing the path are quite different. I thought I had a deep understanding of the teachings. Indeed, I have had many blessed experiences along the way, but I was not prepared for the startling new insights and revelations that came to me.

Those insights and revelations constituted a sacred gift within the gift of my experience in 2009. It truly shifted the core beliefs of my life and resulted in an expansive ability to love unconditionally in ways that were not available to me at the beginning of my sojourn.

Let me take you on a whirlwind tour of where I have been, pulling together the highlights of the journey, to give you a sampling of where you are about to travel with these written words as your guide. May you open your consciousness to the thought that there is truly only One entity reverberating through the entire universe and that because of that awareness in your crown chakra, you will know *you are never alone.*

You will explore the corridors of your mind, knowing that when you see God in the details of your day from a higher consciousness, you can avoid becoming stuck in the illusions of the Monkey Mind in your third eye chakra. You will became aware that all your choices in thought, word, and deed, when aligned with the Truth of who you are, will reflect your connection to that Oneness in your throat chakra. You will learn that your heart chakra is the place of your spiritual birth where you experience how beloved you are by Spirit, allowing you to radiate compassion and unconditional love to all beings. This is where you will give spiritual birth to all the wisdom so freely given by Spirit along your way, knowing that you will need to nurture it as a loving parent would until the wisdom matures into the guiding principles that will navigate your external life in your lower three chakras.

The new wisdom revealed to you will become infused in your soul, shifting the compass of your life and affecting how you interact with your interior and exterior worlds. You will shift the foundation of what you choose to include in your sense of self from the values of the exterior world to the Truth of your internal sanctuary. You will know in your solar plexus chakra the detrimental effects on your soul of compromising that Truth. You will discover where to go to receive creative inspiration and know that you can experience the presence of Spirit through each of your physical senses. You will become aware of how much relationships inform your soul's journey of illumination in your sacral chakra. Last, but not least (by any stretch of our imaginations), you will become aware in your root chakra that you are part of the same tribe of humanity and are one with all creation, with no need to be fearful. You will realize that you end up where you started: What is in the One is in the whole, the message of the crown chakra. What a journey!

Here are a few travel tips to remember along the way as you move along on this continual journey of illumination of your soul. Know that Spirit will always respond to your heart-felt prayers with compassion and unconditional love for you and will shower you with Divine grace. Keep in mind that the answers you receive may not be what you were hoping for and that those answers will come at a time of Spirit's choosing, but never doubt that your answer will come. Eckhart Tolle, spiritual teacher and author has told us, "The power is in you. The answer is in you. And you are the answer to all your searches: you are the goal. You are the answer. It's never outside." Tolle is speaking about the Truth of who you are, not about your egoic self, and that Truth always contains the answer to all your searching.

When you do not feel grounded or feel unsettled and possibly fearful, go within to that place where the still, small voice resides that has called to you so many times. Center yourself in the peace and harmony you have previously touched. Know that it is always there within you. Do not focus on the imbalance you think surrounds you; this is the illusion of chaos. Consciously shift to the infinite array of choices you will discover along your journey when going within to ask for Divine revelation. Always remember that you may choose unconditional love and peace to replace your unbalanced energy. Look at the illusion you are in through the eyes of your heart and not of your egoic mind.

Once you are centered, reverently ask to have the place where you are not aligned with the Truth of who you are to be illuminated. Listen with an open heart for the answer, without judgment. That answer will redirect you back to your path. Take notes in a journal and review those notes to remind yourself of the wisdom that was hidden in previous times when you were feeling the same way. Reassure yourself that that wisdom will now enable you to navigate through the current challenge. Think of how much smoother challenges will be now, knowing where to go when you are searching for answers.

You will learn that Divine grace and guidance have and always will lead you on your soul's journey. This knowing will allow you to go easy on yourself and the others around you who are catching up to your new evolving being. The relationships you develop with fellow soul sojourners will support you along the way.

Self-"excavation" is usually an arduous task. Even though no one can make your journey for you, you need not fend for yourself throughout your odyssey. The classic traps that have been described by souls who have traversed this path throughout the ages are fear and desire. Saint Teresa of Avila referred

to them as reptiles that have invaded your peace. You will learn
how to keep a watchful eye for these invaders that slip in when
you are centered in your egoic mind and not in your heart.

The reading of this book will be the easy part of your soul's
journey of illumination, the passive part of the journey. The
next part will not be nearly as easy. It is the active part, and it
involves putting what resonated with your soul not only into
your consciousness, but into your physical world, which is a
more challenging task.

The Truths and practices that I will share with you from
the sages and mystics with whom I am most familiar will not
at first be effortless or painless for you to grasp. Yet they are
exceedingly necessary to guide you. Put into place in your life,
they will keep you from taking the wrong fork in the road.
"Wrong" here means a longer way to get to where you want
to go, for all roads take most of us within ourselves eventually. However, as the saying goes, "You can go by wisdom or
by woe." The fourteenth-century Persian poet Shamsuddin
Muhammad Hafiz gives us a similar way of contemplating the
journey in a portion of his poem *A Divine Invitation*. Daniel Ladinsky's translation captures the poem's message beautifully in this stanza:

> *We can come to God*
> *Dressed for dancing.*
> *Or*
> *Be carried on a stretcher*
> *To God's ward.*

After all, we are all heading to the destination of returning
to the Source of our being.

Not only will this arduous journey be difficult for you, it will be just as arduous, if not more so, for those around you. You have the benefit at least of having some idea about what you are doing, but those around you will likely be clueless, especially if they have no experience with the "going within" odyssey. There may be casualties along the way. You may lose some relationships. For some of you, the journey now is no longer optional; for others, it will be the wrong time or season. Seasons change and come around again, so there will be innumerable opportunities to gather your intentions and sincere desires to launch your discovery of Self.

No purchased tickets are required for this journey, and there are no security checks. All are welcomed with open arms.

The Metaphor of Water
as the Flow of Divine Grace

In the prelude and introduction of this book, I use the metaphor of water for the Divine grace that I was given that morning as I was smudging. Divine grace is the power that removes the obstacles that stand in the way of our soul's illumination. That power intricately weaves its way into our consciousness. The illuminating process reveals the wisdom of wholeness that is within our being not yet unveiled, for many of us, yearning to be discovered. Each and every one of us has been touched by Divine grace in very individualized and intimate ways.

As we follow the path of this metaphor, we will have a deeper understanding of how Divine grace has affected our life, and our personal hidden wisdom will be revealed. One major Truth of this wisdom is the realization that we were never alone and that we are indeed One with our Creator. We will become aware that there is a very different way to interact with our life's journey, hand in hand with our soul on its journey of illumination.

The metaphor of water has been used throughout the centuries to describe something that is ineffable and one that many of us are all familiar with. Artists, composers, authors, poets, mystics, and others have used the metaphor of water to convey the indescribable experience they have had with something out of the ordinary. When anyone tries to relate a profound experience to someone, they often begin by saying "it was like" because there are no words that can capture the experience; then they proceed to describe something they think the person they are speaking with can resonate with. Metaphors that use water as the vehicle of conveyance of a concept are plentiful: it is like the immensity of an ocean, the stillness of a pond, the flow of a river, or the depth of a well, and so on. Saint Teresa of Avila used the metaphor of water to relate the Source of her being. She spoke of drinking from the well of God, which never goes dry. In some cases this metaphor of water has been used by humans to describe their experiences and understanding of what their culture refers to as the unnamable: Allah, Creator, God, Source, Spirit, Waken Tanka, or Yahweh, to name a few.

Water also seems to be a substance that evokes a stirring of deep emotion within us and is probably why so many beings have used it as a metaphor. More than likely, you can reflect on an experience you have had, something beyond what mere words can describe, when you have been drawn into the enchantment of water. Have you had the experience of sitting by a river or stream of water observing a leaf or feather being carried along by the flow of the water's current and wondered where it might be going or where it will end up and realized that you were on a similar journey of "unknowing" in your life? Or maybe you have had the opportunity to observe a body of water that appeared to be still and calm, unaware of the strong current running deep under its surface until you heard the roar of its powerful waterfall as it fell free to the ground below and recognized the times in your life that you were in a free fall and did not see it coming. How about the immensity of an ocean that resonates with our inner sense of expansion that you cannot describe?

Do you compare events in your life's journey to bodies of water, some twisting and turning at times, some slowly and gracefully meandering with no view of its destination? Or do you relate more to an ocean that reaches the cliffs and then crashes against the inflexible barrier of that landmass? Maybe you have experienced your life as moving along on a fairly lovely ride on a wandering stream, a few bumps along the way, maybe a slight change in direction because of some debris that made its way into your stream, but you think you have successfully navigated your way around the obstacle. Or did you? Some of us experience life as a tumultuous white water rapids river ride with clenched fists and white knuckles. We have all met those whose lives appear — and I emphasize the word *appear* — to flow at just the right speed and direction at all times.

Although our ride has been on the stream of life, most of us come to a place where our stream comes to a still point, if even for an ever so brief period. The movement of our lives stops. It takes a while for most of us even to become aware that something has changed in the flow of our lives. As stillness seeps into our consciousness, we may be somewhat uncomfortable with the inactivity of this space. We start to question what is going on and may explore our journey so far and how we reached this place. When we ask that question, be assured, the journey of our souls has begun in earnest.

SEARCHING FOR ANSWERS

We are instinctively becoming aware of an emerging desire to have the course of our lives move in a significantly different way since we know we are not "there" yet, wherever "there" is. We inquire of ourselves if we have made "it" yet. We have heard about "it," read books about "it," attended workshops on "it," but we have not yet experienced the "it" that has completed us.

We may begin to be nagged by thoughts like, "Is this all there is?" We feel within us that something is missing, but we cannot quite get a handle on what we are reaching for. Many of us are not aware that this yearning is the call for an alignment of ourselves with the Truth of who we really are. We intuitively know we are a part of something bigger than what we are currently experiencing ourselves to be, but we are unsure of what that something is. We look around in an effort to get our bearings, comparing our current surroundings with places and circumstances we have known before. We long to go back to some of those places, even though we know that is not possible. We are aware that we cannot stand in the same river of days gone by as all rivers are continually changing. This awareness is the underlying principle of the well-worn phrase "We can never go back home."

Upon reflection, some of us become aware of how relieved we are no longer to be stuck in episodes of the chaotic whirlpools we once called our life. This can be the dawning of our awakening as we begin to explore and question where we are in our lives and where we think we want to be. We know there is more to life because we have had ever so brief touches of "it" now and then. When we have shared our times on the "wondering what life is about" theme, we may have been told by very well meaning people to "get over" ourselves and move on. But we have come to a place in our lives where the yearning to be connected to something deep within our being can no longer be silenced. For many of us, including myself, we ask, "How could I have ended up here, yet again?" It seems the harder some of us try to redirect the flow of our course and take control of our lives, the more we keep ending up in a very similar place with an intuitive knowing that this is definitely not the "it" we were searching for.

Have you not found yourself at a loss for words when someone has asked you to describe what you are searching for? Have you heard yourself say, "I don't know, but I'll know it when I find it," or "I'll know it when I feel it"? Like most of us, I have looked for fulfillment in many different places. Driven by this sense of restlessness, I have looked outside myself to find the things, people, places — you name it — to fill the void in my heart and soul. Now, however, I know that the only place to look for wholeness is within, and I call on the gift of Divine grace to lead me to the Source of my yearning and searching.

To begin the journey of reuniting with the Oneness, the Truth of who we are, we must be open to the space within that has been calling us, allowing ourselves to feel any discomfort or, for some of us, pain that our separation has created. We must have the courage to follow the call of our soul, the awareness that we are not yet whole. Once we are committed to this path of self-discovery, we must open our hearts and minds to a different way of being, experiencing our vulnerability and fear of the unknown. From a place deep within our being, we need to ask humbly for help and guidance and allow ourselves to be carried by the flow of Divine grace to our Source, with no preconditions or expectations. We must have trust and faith that we will be embraced with unconditional love beyond anything we have experienced before. After all, have we not come to this fork in the road many times before, hoping the direction we took would have a different outcome than the well-worn paths we had previously traversed? Different set of characters or surroundings present maybe, but pretty much the same old "me" was reaching for that infamous "it" at the end of the trail.

"What's wrong with me?" we demand of ourselves, but no answers come. These deep feelings of despair and sense of abandonment constitute what some refer to as the "dark night of the soul", which is the title of an infamous poem by St. John of the Cross, a sixteen-century Spanish mystic. The poem was based on his arduous journey within his soul. Joseph Campbell, an American mythologist and scholar, has written extensively in *The Hero with a Thousand Faces* about the "hero's journey," again about the individual taking the classic journey within toward transformation of the self. Many familiar stories and myths tell of that journey: Dorothy in *The Wizard of Oz*, Luke Skywalker in *Star Wars*, Simba in *The Lion King*, Ulysses in Homer's *Odyssey*, and many, many more. The theme is the same, with great anguish being the catalyst that puts us on the road of discovering the Truth of who we are. When we face this abyss we are still not conscious that the fear and isolation we are experiencing is an essential part of our transformational process.

If you have this book in your hands, you are obviously seeking something more for your life than you are living now. You must be one of those souls searching for more awareness of the Truth of your being, as I doubt you would have ended up reading even this far in this book otherwise. I sincerely hope this writing will assist you in some small way on your journey of expanding your awareness of the Truth of who you are.

My intent in offering this book is to share the experiences of my soul's journey thus far, in the hope that maybe something that I have experienced may shed some small ray of light on a struggle you may be encountering in your life at this time or this sharing may be a catalyst to deepen your quest to become more whole. This is not a scholarly work; it is an experiential work of sharing the gifts that have been given to me. I will be using many different names for God throughout this book, such as Creator, Source, and Spirit.

Please use the word that is most meaningful to you and that describes the designer of creation as you know it. I will also be sharing my understanding of the teachings of many great souls who have guided me on my way. My hope is that as you read and participate in the reflections I suggest, the knowledge and wisdom you gain from your interior work on this soul journey will benefit you on your voyage of transformation and ultimately will benefit the universe itself, as we are all One.

Please keep a journal with you as you read this book as there will be reflections I will ask you to participate in. It is essential to go deeply within your own being when doing work of a transformative nature and then to write about thoughts and feelings that arise in you. You will also want to capture any new insights and wisdom that will be revealed to you as a result of reflective and contemplative moments.

My experience is that when I do not write about sacred gifts in the moment, many times I lose the subtle nuances of the gift from the Divine that I received.

CHAPTER 1

OPENING TO THE FLOW OF DIVINE GRACE

Self is the only prison that can ever bind the soul.
— *Henry Van Dyke*

Man stands in his own shadow and wonders why it's dark.
— *Zen proverb*

A FEW YEARS BACK I took the proverbial "leap of faith" into the abyss out of desperation. After quite an extensive journey within that included a great deal of soul searching, I became aware that what had been guiding me along the tumultuous twists and turns of my sojourn was indeed Divine grace. I had a preconceived idea that if God was communicating with me, I would know it for sure. I thought it would be like being blinded by a most powerful light or hearing a voice from on high that I had been told about in my early childhood religious education classes. I will share some of the wisdom I have come in contact with and what I have learned along the endless road I am traveling.

Divine Grace

Divine grace is a power that cannot be literally described. It really is beyond words. I can only share my limited understanding of it and my experiences with its power, profound compassion, and unconditional love. Divine grace is a glorious gift from Spirit that is given freely and unconditionally to all, a signature of Spirit's presence. Whether we are able to sense it or identify that we have been blessed by it when it flows into our lives in an ever so subtle way is the question to ask ourselves. For some of us, it is only with reflection on the experiences we have had, and well after the event has occurred, that we become aware that God had indeed touched our souls.

Think of an experience you had that seemed inconsequential at the time, perfectly ordinary, but managed to get your attention in a slightly different manner than most of the everyday occurrences in your life. You still remember that "ordinary" moment to this day. Have you ever revisited that seemingly ordinary experience and questioned why, of all the millions of events that have occurred in your life, that moment still remains with you? Reflect on that once-thought-of "ordinary" moment, and in retrospect you may discover that it contained an "extraordinary" message from your soul.

Divine grace can also be a force that rocks you out of your unconsciousness and fills you with ecstasy. Being blessed with Divine grace can leave you with an overwhelming sense of humility, your mind perplexed in its thinking of what you could have possibly done to be touched in this way. It is not an experience of your senses, mind, or body, but one of your soul. The experience of being permeated with God's presence is beyond your limited understanding and reasoning ability.

Being touched by Divine grace is a transformational event that comes unannounced and of a time of God's choosing. You cannot make the experience happen. In many cases it takes time to realize the effect it has had on you, but one thing is for sure: you can never, ever forget the experience. It is a momentous connection with the innate Divinity of creation that makes you aware that there is so much more to God than you can possibly imagine or grasp with your limited mind. Yet you are indeed a part of it. Divine grace carves a path in your soul to the Truth and sets afire your quest for union with the Divine. Mystics from all spiritual traditions have spoken or written about it, but I imagine they were left with a sense of frustration, as it is impossible to give a clear and concise description of something as profound as Divine grace.

Some of you may be thinking, "I really have not received any Divine grace." Yet I assure you that you have, and as you move through this book you will be able to identify the distinct way that the gift of Divine grace has been given to you. Each of us receives Divine grace and guidance in a different format, but we all are blessed with those gifts. The challenge is to recognize them as gifts and to allow them to transform our lives.

The question to ask regarding these messages is not whether the message given was "Divine guidance," but what will we do with the new awareness we have received. Our interpretation of the message will determine the choices we make in response to the gift and therefore the consequences of those choices. Our lives and the lives of others will be directly affected as a result of our actions. We will learn to trust Divine guidance as we ask and open ourselves further to the flow of Divine grace into our lives.

Just as early, mysterious signs of life begin anew with spring without our knowing, when we are not conscious of its signs, we may be unaware of the presence of Divine grace. Most of us are so caught up in our daily activities that we may not slow down enough to sense the delicate stirring of its presence. We may never have noticed that Divine grace has surrounded us throughout our lives. Its presence and essence are not something that can be taught the way spelling rules, mathematical principles, and theories of quantum physics are taught. We are sometimes not even aware that it was Divine grace that played an intimate role in a very challenging time in our lives until years later in a journey of reflection. However, once we begin to sense that something beyond us is intervening in our lives and we honor that presence, we will never be able to deny its presence again. Our awareness quickens to the essence of this ever so subtle movement within our souls. Little do we realize that the awakening has already begun; we were simply not yet awake to its stirrings within.

Take some time to reflect on the following poem by James Dillet Freeman, which attempts to describe the constant presence of God in our lives.

I Am There
Do you need me?
I am there.
You cannot see Me, yet I am the light you see by.
You cannot hear Me, yet I speak through your voice.
You cannot feel Me, yet I am the power at work in your hands.

THE TRANSFORMATIONAL PROCESS

In our unconscious state we are similar to caterpillars crawling along, so many legs to coordinate to get them to where they think they need to go. Similarly, our interior vision is limited because we are so busy trying to control and coordinate our lives that we miss the subtleties of the presence of Divine grace. We are consumed with survival, with what is next to accomplish, what direction or action we should take to get us where we need to be and obtain what we think we need. We may believe we can obtain what we need by dominating and manipulating circumstances at any cost to achieve our desires and be in control of our lives.

Life at this point in our consciousness is pretty simple. We have it all figured out. Things are pretty much black and white, and we judge those around us who do not see life according to our beliefs. We are certain that we are right and that those who do not agree with us are simply wrong. Yet at times something feels slightly off center, and we may attribute that uneasy feeling to not trying hard enough or not being focused enough. With sheer determination we plow ahead and leave a wake behind us. We are oblivious to the consequences of our actions as we have been many times before. We move on and do not ask, "What was that all about?" never pausing to consider what we have done. We tell ourselves, "Keep moving, stay focused, for God's sake! What's wrong with you anyway?" And on we go until the next time our soul whispers that it wants to be heard. When we finally surrender, knowing that what we are continually doing is not getting us where we think we need to be, we are able to ask for assistance. We get a sense of what Albert Einstein's definition of insanity means, "Insanity: doing the same thing over and over again and expecting different results."

Again the feeling of uneasiness rises, but this time more powerfully. It gets our attention. This time it cannot be ignored. This time we pause long enough to ponder what is really going on, and we begin to realize that we really do not have all the answers. The next step in the process is somewhat similar to the cocoon stage of the caterpillar: we go within, searching for answers, although we are not protected from everything outside ourselves the way the silk cocoon protects the caterpillar. We find ourselves feeling isolated within, still unaware of the Divine grace that is guiding us through a most difficult process — the process of not knowing what to do next. We can no longer deny that we are off track, confused about our direction.

Our answers are not so black and white after all; many more shades of gray have entered our expanding field of thought. We become aware that we are losing our bearings, and we begin to doubt our core beliefs. Where is this sense of bewilderment coming from? "How did I get here?" we ask. At this point in our journey, we are not aware that this sense of being lost is essential for our transformation to begin. We find ourselves more alone than we have ever been before. We certainly would not consider this state of utter confusion to be a gift of Divine grace and that this very unsettling sense of not knowing is a wake-up call.

In its own time and when we are stripped of our previous futile attempts to control our world and have asked for answers as to why things are as they are, we have unknowingly opened a space for Divine grace to flow more freely into our consciousness and our hearts, like the dawn of a new day.

With newfound courage and the beginning awareness of our connection to the Truth of who we are, we release some of our old beliefs and embrace the sense of true peace that is beginning to unfold within our being. Our vision is expanding; we are no longer crawling on the ground focused on survival or lost in the darkness of a cocoon. We are beginning to view our lives from a much different prospective. Our wings are beginning to take form, and we are preparing to take flight.

This transformational process is not a linear experience with a beginning, middle, and end. We are not caterpillars that experience a specified period in a cocoon and then poof! — We are butterflies! I have experienced transformation to be a recurring process, usually different every time. From what friends have shared with me regarding their experiences with the transformational effects of Divine grace, the process is also different for everyone. On occasion, Divine grace announces itself in a manner that leaves the person without doubt that it has intervened dramatically in his or her life. These people become aware that they are in touch with awe, a place within they have never encountered before, instructing them to go in a definitive direction. On most other occasions, Divine grace is much more subtle until our consciousness is attuned to its presence.

As I stated earlier here, for some the process can begin with just a wisp of awareness that something is amiss in our lives. For others, it is a genuine crisis that can be followed by a profound going within, and for others, a crisis situation brings them to their knees. Whatever shape the process takes, we always come out the other end as different people, sometimes for the better and sometimes temporarily for the worse. On and on it goes, our soul beckoning us to become aware of the Truth of who we are. Over and over we begin the journey, but somehow it is not quite the same each time because we have received Divine guidance along our way and have retained that wisdom in our souls. Each time that we embark on the journey within, the flow of

Divine grace clears more of our resistance from our path toward becoming more aligned with the Truth of who we are. Thus, we show up in our lives in a slightly more present way. Again similar to the flow of water, rivers can carve canyons in mountains. Divine grace clears mountains of debris to clear the path to our souls. Divine grace's force permeates our souls with the knowing that we are most certainly not alone. This is the journey of illumination, with the final destination of union with the One.

I now believe that it is impossible not to be surrounded with Divine grace, whether or not we are aware of its presence. Within the past few years I have reflected deeply on my life and have become aware that Divine grace has always protected me and guided me on my soul's journey. There have been times in my life that I have labeled as tumultuous episodes, where I felt as though I were a lost soul and fully alone. I now know that there is nowhere to go that Divine grace is not present. It is a matter of opening oneself to its presence and becoming aware of it yourself.

But "how do you do this?" you ask. I truly wish I had an easy and simple answer for you. I know for me, asking with an open heart in reverent prayer and becoming as still as I possibly can within my being allows me to become more and more aware of the power that Divine grace has had in my life.

A Course in Miracles, a large work published in 1976 that was channeled by Helen Schucman and scribed by William Thetford, both professors of medical psychology at Columbia University's College of Physicians and Surgeons, states that "a universal theology is impossible, but a universal experience is not only possible but necessary." It further states that this "universal experience" is the knowing that you have been in God's presence or that you have experienced union with God, the

Oneness of the universe that so many mystics, sages, and individuals have experienced quite unexpectedly. Some of these blessed beings have written about their experiences to guide us along our way. I hope you find something in this writing that will fuel your desire to know the Divine presence of God.

Spiritual Alchemy

We will spend a portion of our time on this journey together exploring our past to uncover the gifts we did not recognize at the time they were given. These periods of reflection will assist us in awakening our inner wisdom instead of dwelling on what we have once viewed as pain and suffering. We may think we have successfully navigated around the debris in the stream of our lives or planted the experiences in a deep hole, never to see the light of day again, putting them behind us. In most cases, however, they unexpectedly sprout up. By that I mean that we are unconscious of the enormous toll they continue to have on our lives and souls because they remain alive and well. We will delve into the depths of these experiences with the skills of a spiritual alchemist and retrieve the golden wisdom these leaden experiences contain.

Alchemy is described as a chemical philosophy that attempts to change a base metal into gold. One of my goals in this book is to transform some of the experiences you have had in your life, the ones you label as negative. We will go within our beings, reverently asking for Divine grace to pierce through that negativity and reveal the golden wisdom that it contains. To retrieve this latent wisdom, we need to go deep within.

We will open our hearts and souls to Divine grace, releasing the fear and false beliefs that keep us from connecting with our souls. Part of the process of transformation is understanding how that wisdom affects the interaction between the energies of the *chakras* and the energies of the world outside yourself. You will then be able to use that understanding, revealed wisdom, and new wisdom you will discover, to navigate your soul's journey in alignment with a new life compass.

You will discover that many of the events that you previously experienced with great sadness or fear at the time were gems in the rough. These as-yet unrevealed gems have the potential to offer you a clearer perception of events once described as painful, resulting in the ability to be more present in your life today. You will be able to move into your future knowing, from your own experience that things truly do work according to a Divine order for the greatest good. Your inner wisdom will reveal that Divine grace has guided you along the way and was always present throughout your life. This is captured well by a poem by Mary Stevenson that many of you may already be familiar with:

FOOTPRINTS IN THE SAND
One night I dreamed I was walking along the beach with the Lord.

Many scenes from my life flashed across the sky.

In each scene I noticed footprints in the sand.

Sometimes there were two sets of footprints,

other times there were one set of footprints.

This bothered me because I noticed

that during the low periods of my life,

when I was suffering from

anguish, sorrow or defeat,

I could see only one set of footprints.

So I said to the Lord,

"You promised me Lord,

that if I followed you,

you would walk with me always.

But I have noticed that during
the most trying periods of my life
there have only been one
set of footprints in the sand.
Why, when I needed you most,
you have not been there for me?"
The Lord replied,
"The times when you have
seen only one set of footprints
is when I carried you."

The journey of the illumination of the soul, as I noted before, is a process, but by no means a sequential one, many times feeling more like two steps forward and one step back. Many times we are unaware of the changes that are occurring, not unlike a farmer and a newborn calf: A farmer found himself in a position that he needed to lift a newborn calf over an obstacle so it could receive its nutrients. Every day he faithfully lifted this calf over the obstacle so the calf could eat. One day, someone passing by stopped and asked the farmer, "How is that you have the strength to lift a cow?" The farmer only then realized the calf was no longer a calf. The farmer had not noted the calf's incremental weight gain because he was accustomed to lifting the "calf," which had become a cow.

You may find that you do not notice the changes within yourself for quite some time, similar to the caterpillar's myopic view of self. It may take someone else remarking how surprised he or she was because of the way that you responded to a stressful situation in a way that was not characteristically "like you." You become gradually in touch with a new compass of your life, and this influences how you interact with the external world — you interact rather than react. Inner peace arises in your soul. This is the most precious gift that anyone can receive.

Illumination

When I use the word *illumination* in regard to the journey of our souls, simply put, I am referring to the conscious awareness of being connected, transcendent of self, with the Source from which we were created. This consciousness is not undertaken by our intellects. Quite the opposite. It is the process of our hearts opening to the presence of the Infinite within our souls. Illumination is an experiential occurrence by which we feel the awareness of Spirit's presence, allowing us to experience precious moments of the nature of our being.

Enlightenment represents the end of the false belief that we are separate from the Source of our creation, the point when all fear is dissolved. Spiritual masters who have become aware of the Source of their beings or souls and have the ability to remain in that consciousness are called enlightened. Their awareness is consistently "in the light." Their enlightenment comes from union with the Divine within their being, not from the world outside themselves. It may be, however, that the external world will serve as a catalyst for flashes of illumination. When, for example, we are driven deeply within ourselves by an external event, we may touch the luminous light of our souls, or we may experience these brief glimpses of illumination during periods of reverent prayer, contemplation, or reflection.

For most of us, illumination is an infrequent and inconsistent occurrence as we move through the journey of our lives. If we were to experience the full force of enlightenment, it would overwhelm most of us. Many mystics and sages throughout the ages have written extensively on their experiences of illumination and its overwhelming effects, often rendering them speechless and powerless to describe what they experienced. Two examples of enlightened beings are Buddha and Christ, who had the ability to remain in union with Oneness consistently and consciously.

A few words of clarification here before we move on. In this book I make frequent references to the Truth, with a capital *t*. The reason for this is that Truth is something that never changes, just as the earth rotates around the sun and birth comes before death. No one can change the Truth; however, Truth does change people. Something can be true at one time but not at other times. The outside temperature one day is often different from the next day's temperature; both are true temperatures so therefore they are true but not Truth. Thus, each time you read the word *Truth*, know that I am referring to something that does not change. Likewise, I will also capitalize many other words throughout the book: Creator, One, Source, Spirit, and the like. Whenever you note a capitalized word that is not usually capitalized, know that I am referring to God or the Truth of who we are.

THE CHAKRAS

In chapters two through eight, I focus on chakras. There are seven major chakras. We will explore how Divine grace brings illumination and empowerment to each chakra's wisdom, offering us options and choices as we move forward on the journey of our souls toward illumination. Indian yogis were the first people to identify the chakra system many thousands of years ago. Many authors through the ages describe the chakra system as comprising individual vortices of energy that receive and transmit energy. These vortices are located along the spinal column from the base of our spines to above the crown of our heads. Although chakras are described as individual energy centers, they work together as a whole system. Some authors have described additional chakras but I focus on the seven most familiar ones in this book.

These energy centers, when illuminated by Divine grace, assist us in balancing our physical world with our spiritual world. As we grow in our ability to incorporate the wisdom and knowledge that each chakra contains, our consciousness expands and our alignment with the universal laws of creation strengthens. Each chakra holds wisdom that assists us in navigating our lives through the challenges we all inevitably encounter along the way on the journey of our souls toward illumination. Just as important as aligning ourselves with the "light side" of the chakra energy patterns, we must be continually alert to the shadow, or to what is sometimes referred to as the dark side, of these energy centers as well. The illuminated energy of the chakras will expand our awareness of our connection to the "One" and consequently guide our choices in thought, word, and deed with unconditional love, while the shadow energy of the chakras will constrict our awareness through fear and guide us based on the principle of the small "one": me and what's in it for me.

Each chakra does not have a clear-cut definitive boundary where its energy pattern begins and the other starts. The chakras function as an interrelated system, the energy of each influencing the others. Most important for us to understand is that these energy patterns are continually providing us with input from our environment. The energy patterns also affect how we respond to our environment, physically, emotionally, and spiritually. It is up to us to actively decide to align with the Divine grace that is constantly available to guide us in our ability to interpret the energetic message that the chakras are sending. How we interpret the message will determine all our choices in thought, word, and deed, which will directly affect our lives, the lives of all the others we interact with, and the universe itself. I present the chakras from the top down, as opposed to the traditional presentation from the bottom up. I describe how Divine grace flows down through the chakras, illuminating aspects of each chakra's energies, as this is the inspiration I received. What follows is a truly brief description of the individual chakra patterns. I hope the description will give you a basic understanding of our interior landscape and what aspects of our interior and exterior world each chakra influences. At the beginning of each chapter, I also give a brief review of the specific chakra's pattern. As we travel on the path of our souls' journey through the chakras, always keep in mind that the chakras constitute a system rather than individual parts.

THE CROWN CHAKRA

The crown chakra, located just above the crown of the head, is the chakra that connects us to universal, or pure consciousness, an awareness of the One and that we are contained in that One. This experience can happen in an instant through the Divine grace of Spirit uniting us with the Oneness of cosmic consciousness and takes us beyond our physical world. Duality and illusion are no longer present in the lives of beings that are able to hold this consciousness consistently. As I have said, these souls are enlightened beings. These are beings who chose to remain in their physical bodies for the sake of humanity, to teach and enlighten others. However, enlightened souls may choose to drop their physical bodies when they become enlightened and merge into the Oneness.

The experience of Divine grace here is life altering; it shifts our perception of the limited finite world to the infinity of the Divine world. Spiritual practices such as meditation and prayer can certainly help to create a receptive space for enlightenment, but people who were not consciously on a spiritual path have received a profound, transforming spiritual experience of Oneness. The crown chakra becomes illuminated with the awareness of what is best for the whole rather than just for the self. This consciousness benefits not only the self but all, as the Truth that we are all *One* has been revealed. This is the consciousness that is beyond there being a subject and an object; there is just the One.

THE THIRD EYE CHAKRA

The third eye chakra, located behind the center of the forehead, is where the soul experiences its object, the object of all its yearnings and searching: God. In the Hindu tradition, this chakra is depicted as a lotus blossom with two petals: the individual and God. When this chakra is illuminated, the vision of the internal and external world is beyond duality or opposites. This is the realm of spiritual vision and awareness, where we go beyond our individual desires and are aligned with what is for the good of all. This is the realm of the mystics and sages. The illumination of this energy center dramatically changes the trajectory of our lives.

The changes we make in our lives as a result of this experience with Divine grace are based on the belief that we are indeed all One, no longer centered in what is best for the individual.

When the third eye chakra is not fully illuminated, it is connected to the intellect and the mind. This energy pattern is associated with the rationalization of the world around us by our minds and our futile attempts to use our reason to know why things are as they are, which is attached to the belief that we are separate from the One, which is also the illusion of duality. This illusion therefore results in our narrow perspective of reality: that there is you and me. Our separatist thought pattern puts us in a position to dance with the energy of duality. And what a dance we do! The belief of separation is so potent it can control our thoughts and the basic understanding of our individual world. Divine grace sheds light on our gross misinterpretation of the world around us and has the profound ability to shift our awareness into a higher consciousness.

The Throat Chakra

The throat chakra, located in the center of the throat, is associated with our personal wills, the choices we make in life in all our thoughts, words, and deeds. These choices affect everyone involved in the decisions we make and all the other beings with whom we interact. Our beliefs have a pervasive effect on our wills, and they affect which level of consciousness we choose to apply to all the decisions we make in our lives. This chakra is also associated with our ability to communicate, not only with others but with ourselves, with what we tell ourselves. Divine grace can shift the energy of our personal will to the Divine: Your will versus my will.

When not illuminated, the throat chakra energy pattern can shrink our lives to the world according to us. Our choices will then be based on how to get what we want at any cost, without regard to how our choices affect those around us. We communicate from a place of self-centered interests and are willing to speak untruths if that will get us where we think we need to be.

THE HEART CHAKRA

The heart chakra, located in the heart region, between the breasts, is ground zero for all our emotions. It is the energy center where compassion and unconditional love of self and others are generated. The emotion of fear rather than compassion will be the ruler of our thoughts, words, and deeds when we are not aligned with the Truth of who we are. When we humbly ask for Divine grace to illuminate our hearts from a place of purity of this desire, we are blessed with the capacity to love others and ourselves unconditionally and radiate compassion to all. The heart chakra is the center where we give birth to compassion and unconditional love. With the illumination of Divine grace, we have the ability to act from a place of forgiveness, and reverence for all life.

The shadow energy of the heart chakra is anger, an inability to forgive, and revenge. Again, the emotion of fear becomes the ruler of our thoughts, words, deeds, and emotions when we are not aligned with the Truth of who we are, and we will consequently live our lives from a lonely and resentful space.

THE SOLAR PLEXUS CHAKRA

The solar plexus chakra, located an inch or two above the naval, is the center of our sense of self, also known as self-esteem. Here we choose the criteria on which we will base our self-esteem, our inner wisdom of the Truth of who we are, or the external world with its ever-changing standard of what makes us "good enough" in the eyes of this world. Divine grace sheds light on our inner wisdom, which results in a sense of wholeness and strength.

The solar plexus chakra is also the center of our intuition, the "gut" feeling — with the emphasis on *feeling*— we have when we sense that something is either aligned or not aligned with the

Truth of who we are. It is also connected to the awareness that we feel when we have an "Aha!" moment, an episode of insight that resonates with our being. When this chakra is not illuminated, our thoughts, words, and actions will compromise our personal integrity and therefore our soul.

THE SACRAL CHAKRA

The sacral chakra, located a few inches below the naval in the sacrum, is connected to our one-on-one relationships and to the quality of power we bring to those relationships: our light energy or our shadow energy. The sacral energy center holds our sense of individual, or personal power and is highly influenced by our natural "fight or flight" reaction. Divine grace is essential to guide us through the maze of perceived power plays and the fear of being manipulated or humiliated by others. Divine grace is the gift that allows us to view our relationships with the awareness that we are not alone — rather than being driven by fear, resulting in a sense of "me" against "you"— and to interact with others with respect and reverence, as expressions of creation.

Our ability to be creative is also connected to the sacral chakra. When we go within to the space of peace and stillness, we are more likely to align with the creativity of the universe and be inspired by Spirit. This space is also the center of sensuality, a place where our sexual encounters can be infused with unconditional love, allowing us to open ourselves to the vulnerability of intimacy. Many people experience a sense of human oneness, going beyond the duality of "me" and "you," during the height of sexual excitement.

This is the place where we can experience Spirit through our auditory and visual senses as well as our senses of smell, touch, and taste. Creation is full of opportunities to experience the Divine with our senses being the vehicle to enjoy its many pleasures.

THE BASE CHAKRA

The base chakra, sometimes referred to as the root chakra, is located at the base of the spine and is connected to our tribal beliefs. These beliefs can include our family traditions, our tribal spiritual beliefs, our ethnic and cultural traditions, the beliefs of the country we live in, our social-class beliefs, and the like. Our awareness of our attachment to these beliefs and a willingness to explore them deeply will determine whether we choose to expand our vision of the world or remain rigid in our beliefs and ultimately our actions. Divine grace brings the gift of going beyond our limited view of our world to the true belief that we are indeed all One. Imagine how different our lives could be while living from that higher perspective, interacting with others from the belief that we are all One rather than *me* against all the others of the world.

~

Before exploring deeply the effect Divine grace and guidance can have on our energy centers and consequently on our journey, I would like to leave you with a story that reminds me of my own soul's journey and the spirit in which I offer these writings. I am told its origins are in the Muslim Sufi tradition.

A group of people was wandering in the desert for a very long time. They were exhausted and on the brink of dying from thirst. In the distance they saw what appeared to be a monk walking toward them. Their hearts were lifted because they felt they were saved. They believed that surely this holy monk would be able to tell them the way out of the desert. When they were close enough to speak with the monk, one of them said, "Praise God! We have found you. Tell us how we can get out of this desert." The monk lowered his head, knowing they would be disappointed when he replied, "Alas, I wish that I could, but I cannot. However, I can tell you the many ways that I tried to leave the desert but to no avail."

I, and may I be presumptuous in saying that many of you as well, have been looking for a way out of the illusory "desert journey." Moreover, we have felt sure that once found, we would be able to share the many ways we believed would lead us to our goal of inner peace and joy. Alas, we have not found the way. However, the wisdom those experiences hold can change our suffering to joy and our lead to gold, when we reclaim the power we have been Divinely given by becoming spiritual alchemists for our souls, with the power of Divine grace to help us along the way.

For some of you this book will generate a sense of reassurance of the wisdom you are already aware of. For others it may shift your perspectives and perceptions in a way that allows you to have access to the wisdom that is available to you. For still others, this book may create a space inside of you for the first time that allows Spirit to enter into places you have long ago closed to light.

Begin by taking a moment to center yourself, go within to a place of stillness, and then set your intention for this voyage before you embark on this journey into your soul. Reverently ask that your awareness may be infused with Divine grace and guidance so that you may see this journey through the vision of your open heart and not of your wayward mind. Grab your journal to capture the wisdom you will undoubtedly receive. Let us begin the journey of our soul's illumination!

CHAPTER 2

AWARENESS OF THE PRESENCE OF DIVINE GRACE:

THE CROWN CHAKRA

The flow of Divine grace enters our crown chakra and fills it with pure clear water, if you will. Think of the mountain springs in the Himalayas, fresh from the snowmelt, purifying your awareness and consciousness of the Oneness of creation.

Man is a stream whose source is hidden.
— *Ralph Waldo Emerson*

Tat Twam Asi (Thou Art That)
— *Chandogya Upanishad*

IN THIS CHAPTER we delve into the crown chakra, the energy center from which we experience our connection to the Oneness, the all of creation. The Truth of who we are is beyond our comprehension when we try to approach understanding this concept with our intellects. When we receive Divine grace that blesses us with an actual experience of our connection to that Oneness, even for a nanosecond, our perception will never be the same. Mechthild of Magdeburg, a thirteenth-century Beguine mystic, said, "The day of my spiritual awakening was the day I saw — and knew that I saw — all things in God and God in all things."

For just the ever-so slightest fraction of time, the illusion of separation from the One and the smallness of our lives fall away, and we are transported to a completely different level of consciousness: wholeness within. The "it" we have been searching for, that we intuitively knew existed, is now real. There is no turning back. It is like the saying "You can't un-ring the bell." We will never be able to deny that experience of Oneness. Yet it is exceedingly rare for a person to live his or her life consistently here on the earthly plane in the realm of illusion and duality and in that consciousness of Oneness. An enlightened being, as I noted before, is one who is able to sustain the highest level of all consciousness.

There is no distance or space where God is not present in this state of awareness. Joel S. Goldsmith, a New Thought author and teacher, tells us that there is only one relationship and that relationship is the relationship of Oneness. There are no divisions or separation in Oneness. He also said that until we have a relationship with God, we have nothing; but at the very moment we have God, we have the universe itself because there is no such thing as God *and*.

Through the centuries many other beings have attempted to share with us their understanding of Oneness. Humanity has attempted to describe it and has approached this formidable task from different vantage points, ranging from the nonphysical to the physical realm. Mystics and sages from all spiritual traditions have shared their experiences with the Divine from the nonphysical realm of Oneness, leaving guideposts for us as we travel toward our destination of wholeness. To help us along our way, great minds and explorers of science throughout the ages have also strived to share their understanding of the Oneness of our universe from the physical realm by explaining the laws of physics and mathematics that support the reality of the Oneness of the universe.

Joseph Campbell quotes from the Rig Vedic Hindu scriptures in the preface to his book *The Hero with a Thousand Faces:* "Truth is one, the sages speak of it by many names." For me, Divine grace has been the power that set my fervent desire to know God on fire and has nurtured and sustained my deep yearning to grow more in touch with the Oneness of God. The blessings of Divine grace that I have received have further ignited a flame in my soul with an unquenchable craving to be whole. For quite some time, the need to follow this desire has not been optional for me.

This journey of the illumination of the soul is a mystical journey of the true self, revealing itself to us through the power of Divine grace. This grace illuminates our inner shadow, those dark places within that keep us from opening to the sacred space of knowing the Truth of who we are: one with infinite Divinity.

The peace that is beyond human understanding, the sacred place that has been written about by those who have reached it, is experienced in the crown chakra. We become aware that we have truly touched a space within that lets us know we have experienced a sense of being whole. In those precious moments when we experience that deep peace, there is a knowing of a presence and calm that we always want more of. The more we are able to connect with that peace, the more willingly and consciously we open our beings to the place of deep peace that is beyond human understanding.

We feel the stirring of a longing that is beyond desire. We find ourselves yearning more and more for those most blessed moments that are saturated with bliss, joy, and wholeness. The connection to this presence of peace fills that space within us that has been a vacuum. No longer will we be satisfied with the limited things this world has to offer. Although we still take delight in the blessings that are given to us in our external world, our true satisfaction is centered in the wholeness of the Truth of who we are.

AWARENESS OF ONENESS

For ages human beings have attempted to describe Oneness, the place of peace that is beyond understanding as well as the bliss and sense of wholeness that come with it. Yet it is easier to describe Oneness as what it is *not* rather than as what it is. As soon as we put Oneness in thought form, we separate it from itself into subject (soul) and object (God), and we are then back in the world of duality and separation. As human beings, this is the world we primarily live in, the world of duality and separation from the awareness of Oneness. For almost all of us, especially in the West, have been conditioned by our societal norms to accept the illusion of duality as our reality since we arrived in a physical form. Deep within our being, though, there will always be an elusive pull to become whole.

The awareness of our disconnection from the Oneness of creation, which we have all felt at one time or another, can enter our lives as a slight stirring beneath our busy thoughts and life. This slight stirring is barely perceptible when we are focused on our exterior life. It is that faint hint of a presence within that speaks to us of something missing in our lives. We know this presence exists; we cannot describe it or name it, yet its calling is hard to ignore. This concealed presence attempts to break through the clamor of our lives now and then, but most of us are too consumed with the illusion of our lives to explore its source deeply. However, our innate pining for wholeness never gives up on calling us to our true destination, no matter how many times we ignore its beckoning.

How long it takes us to respond to the call from within has to do with our will, the regulator of all the choices we make in our lives. Some of us are awakened to the need to respond to the call by a crisis in our lives. Some wait to the very end of their lives' journey on earth to pay attention to the call. Divine grace may be the initiator of our response to the beckoning of our soul. The manner in which we become connected to Divine grace, the power that unites us with the Oneness of the universe, is of no importance. Yet the moment we become aware of its presence and consciously surrender ourselves to the illuminating power as being the principal guide for our lives, our journey will be changed unimaginably. The unexpected events of our lives are beyond our imagination; they catch us off guard, and the words "you can't make this stuff up if you tried" swirls in our minds.

Divine grace can flood the soul with instantaneous awareness of something beyond our understanding and yet feels as though we have arrived at the place we were always meant to be and have been searching for. Or it can touch us in a gentle way that makes us realize we are not alone. Whatever way Divine grace reveals even a hint of this Oneness, there is no mistaking the true awesomeness of the event. Then the enormous question becomes, how do we live our lives after experiencing this Divine event and stay in that profound awareness? The answer for me is simple: I do not. I occasionally get close to the experience of Oneness that I had many years ago, but I know deep within my being that I did not make it happen nor can I recreate it. It would be foolish to think I could.

I am still enmeshed in the duality of living but have found ways to release some of the attachments that bind me to duality, giving me instants of freedom from my egoic mind, allowing me to move forward in my life from a higher perspective. When we consciously open ourselves in the quest to become the Truth of who we are, we create a more receptive field to receiving Divine grace and to being aware of the Divine grace that always surrounds us. Our yearning and our search become more and more central to our existence and our spiritual path.

James Finley, a clinical psychologist, former Trappist monk, and author says that "the word God is the name we use for everything in the fullness of infinite reality itself." He also teaches that this infinite reality continually reveals itself to us as we open ourselves to its presence. We are not conscious of the fact that we are a part of this "fullness of infinite reality," because we are in the very human state of confusion about and ignorance of our identity. We do receive consolation for this state through our faith in this infinite power that is greater than ourselves. Yet no finite thing, person, or belief will ever be enough to make us feel complete. Only alignment with the Infinite will complete us. So we go about our daily lives, feeling this incompleteness of our love for God, trying to feel our way as we travel on our soul's journey of illumination, the journey toward enlightenment and the fulfilled love and union with the Infinite.

On my spiritual path, I have experienced the axiom of "When the student is ready, the teacher will appear." I have been blessed with the opportunity of being in the presence of some of the most conscious beings on our planet on my quest for spiritual Truth. These teachers have arrived in my life exactly at the right moment, many times without my consciously asking for them.

This is yet another way that Divine grace has revealed itself in my life. In some instances I was unaware of the profound effect they would have on my spiritual path at the time I was with them. Their teachings and my experiences with them slowly evolved within me. They continue to bless me on my spiritual journey to connect with the Oneness of life in ways I could not have imagined at the time of our interactions. The great, radical mystery of life presents us with a wide variety of opportunities to expand our awareness of the Truth of who we are. The question is, are we open to these experiences and are we capable of allowing the experiences to transform us as we push ourselves beyond the limits of who we think we are and into connection with the One?

Although no one can put Oneness into words owing to the constraints of language, various myths, spiritual teachings, and research are especially helpful in attempting to put Oneness in a context to aid our understanding of this profound concept. Those that I share here are some of the most valuable concepts that have crossed my path on my spiritual journey. They have helped me to perceive the essence of the Oneness of the universe. I hope they are of some help to you.

The Native American creation myth of Grandmother Spider is connected to the Hopi, Pueblo, and Navajo nations and describes the Grandmother Spider's web as connecting all life forms of creation. This is the story of the creation of the universe and the weaving of the Web of Life. As Grandmother Spider weaved each life, she did not cut the cord from the previous life form before she began the next creation. Each life form then is connected to the Web of Life. When any one of the life form's vibration changes, those vibrations are transmitted through the entire Web of Life. Each life form is anchored to the Web of Life; therefore, when something in the web is affected, all life forms are affected: nothing is separate.

A Mahayana Buddhist sutra uses the metaphor of Indra's Net to describe the "inter-being," or interpenetration, of all phenomena, meaning that everything contains everything else. An infinite cosmic net stretches out in all directions of the universe, and at each of the net's vertices there is a single multifaceted clear jewel. Each jewel reflects all the other jewels in the net, and the reflection is an endless reflection of infinity. In that endless reflection, the reflection of each jewel reflects all the other jewels in infinite reflections of each. The net of jewels has the same effect as when two mirrors are placed opposite each other, the reflections go on and on without end. Each jewel in Indra's Net represents a consciousness or being. A change in one jewel would be reflected in all the other jewels, demonstrating the interconnectedness of everything in the cosmos, in alignment with the universal law: What is in the One is in the Whole.

Gregg Braden, a best-selling author and previously a senior aerospace computer systems designer, describes the holographic nature of the universe in one of his books, *The DiViNE Matrix*. This book is an extensive exploration of the spiritual and scientific connection of the Oneness of creation. It includes results of scientific experiments that reveal evidence of a web of energy that connects everything in the universe.

Bernard Haisch, Ph.D., an astrophysicist and the author of *The God Theory*, has written one of the most comprehensible analogies of the Oneness of creation. He begins with the discovery that Newton made when he placed a prism so that a beam of sunlight coming through a shutter would shine directly on the prism. Newton observed that on the wall opposite where the sunlight was entering, all the infinite shades of colors of the rainbow appeared, revealing that the pure white light streaming through the shutter contained all the colors of the rainbow, even though it appeared as one light. We are all aware of this phenomenon.

Haisch goes on to explain that in optics today you can view just one of the colors of the white light from a projector simply by placing a filter over the white light, which filters out all the colors except the one you desire. This is the same as viewing a color slide of a photograph by placing it in front of the white light of a projector. The slide acts as a filter, and the result is the projection of the picture on the screen. Haisch explains that this is the process of subtracting colors from the whole pure white light of the projector.

I conceptualize that as we are filters through which we view our manifested, projected world instead of Oneness. Haisch's readings of esoteric traditions brought him to the understanding that such traditions tell us that creation by subtraction is one of the fundamental truths underlying reality. In terms of Haisch's God theory, "these traditions teach that creation of the real (the manifest) involves subtraction from the infinite potential." The "real" in this case is the physical form in the realm of duality.

What we label as reality is based on the same principle of subtracting colors from the pure white light of the projector. We use our individual filters and call this our "reality," or its manifested form. The filters are our beliefs, and consequently how we use those beliefs to view and interact with the world determines our perspective of the world around us. For the most part, the filters are unconscious. Most of us experience ourselves as separate from Oneness as a result of our filters. Consequently, we view everything else as "other," also known as polarity or duality. A body of water has a similar quality to it. A ripple in a stream or a wave in an ocean may appear as a separate entity, but in reality that appearance is just an illusion as it is part of the same body of water. I was struck by the simplicity and clarity of Haisch's analogy for Oneness. Our perspectives of reality are contingent on the filters we place on Oneness. The concept is similar to a spiritual practice of subtraction or elimination that I have followed for many years.

When I was studying Eastern spiritual principles and traveling to India, one of the teachings of the Hindu sage Yajnavalka, in the sacred text of the Upanishads, really resonated within my soul. One of this sage's many teachings was the concept of reaching the Truth, Oneness, by negation or subtraction. This teaching explains Oneness from the opposite end of the spectrum than the esoteric teachings that Haisch referred to. Instead of approaching Oneness from the place of subtracting from Oneness, the pure white light of the projector, to create the manifested, Yajnavalka teaches that we eliminate or subtract the manifested until there is nothing but Oneness.

This teaching is written in the Sanskrit words *neti, neti,* very loosely translated, they mean "not this, not this." In recognizing that the illusion of the manifested is not real by a process of elimination, we eventually come to Oneness. My Western interpretation of this sacred teaching is the disrespectful statement of, "You have to kiss a lot of frogs before you get to the prince," or Oneness.

Neti, Neti: Not This, Not This

In my experience of more than six decades I can claim that I have kissed an enormous number of frogs. Another way of saying this is, after reflection and going within my being, I have identified many aspects of my life that were the illusion "du jour," if you will. The frogs have appeared in my life as religion, people, places, jobs, money, family traditions, personal beliefs, education, and professional credentials. For me, the list goes on and on.

≈

Going Within: Please pause here for a moment and make a list in your journal of your own most memorable "frogs" that did not turn out to be the "princes" you once thought they were. Remember, frogs are not just people. They can be beliefs, religions, or professional credentials for example. Sincerely ask for Divine grace to reveal the truth of those people and situations, and know that in listing them you are on a sacred journey of revelation. Take your time as you identify the frogs that you were sure were the princes you were looking for to fill that empty space in your being. More than likely you were not conscious that that was what the frog represented to you at the time. Nevertheless, you knew that this was "it." I am sure you can come up with at least one belief, experience, or person you were sure was the answer to your longing, but as you evolved, it was revealed to be yet another empty outcome. Looking outside ourselves is always the wrong direction to search for true personal fulfillment. However, empty outcomes and experiences that our ego has labeled as bad or horrific can carry a gem of wisdom for us. With hindsight and a period of deep, prayerful reflection, humbly asking for Divine grace to reveal the wisdom contained in your experiences, you can receive that wisdom into the sacred space of your soul.

Now that you have a list of your own most memorable frogs, close your eyes and open your heart. Allow yourself time to become still and go deep within your soul. Humbly ask for Divine grace to reveal the true message of these experiences. Open yourself to the wisdom that comes from the experiences that you once put in the category of pain and suffering. This is an important reflection because it will put you in touch with your *own* experience on your soul's journey, not something you have read in a book or heard in a workshop. It will be your own experience on the path of *neti, neti*, the process of elimination, or better yet, the process of becoming conscious. Still better, it is the process of illumination and empowerment as you become aware of the Truth of who you are. The prince you are searching for (and, I will be so bold to say, that we are all searching and yearning for and intuitively "know" is there) is the Oneness of which you are a part. This is the meaning of "you are who you are waiting for." Be open to all the answers you receive, especially those that create resistance within your mind and that confront your pride; these answers may be the most authentic.

I hope that you took time to reflect on at least one perceived painful past event that you were not able to recognize as a teachable moment at the time it occurred. Did you experience a shift in your perception of the event or belief? Was the wisdom that that experience contained revealed to you? Did you become aware that things are not always what they appear to be? If your perception did not change, revisit the event or belief later. Continue to ask reverently that Divine grace reveal to you what needs to be revealed, that which will heal the affected part of your soul so that you may become more whole and present in your life.

Write your new "awarenesses" in your journal, and add to them as new awarenesses come to you. The process of writing about your experience can bring more clarity to what has been revealed to you because you need to focus on the experience to know how to put the revelation into words. The writing process also brings your new awareness into the physical world, making the revelations more tangible in your life. You will be able to refer back to your writings and even more may be revealed to you in hindsight and upon reflection. You may even want to share your new awareness with a very trusted friend, someone who will hold your new awareness in sacred trust, whom St. Teresa of Avila referred to as a soul companion, for further exploration. Your sharing may not only help you to heal and become more whole, but it also may be the catalyst of expanded consciousness for your "soul companion."

~

I caution you, however, not to compare your experiences with someone else's experience of a similar situation. As you gain new spiritual insight you will be able to observe and live life from a much different perspective. Henry David Thoreau told us that if we seem out of sync with our companions, it might be because we hear a "different drummer." Remember, you are establishing an intention of receiving Divine guidance from a deep spiritual place and summoning Divine grace in your endeavor to become aware of the Truth of who you are. When you compare your experience with someone who has had a similar traumatic experience, that person may not be able to relate to your new awareness. Your suggestion that the traumatic event in his or her life is really a gift could easily be interpreted as hurtful and insensitive.

Your personal spiritual revelations are for you. You should regard them as sacred messages for your journey. Hold them deep within your soul and share them only with those you trust and feel are traveling on a similar path. I find that whenever I compare anything in my life, tangible or ethereal, with a situation that resembles that of someone else, I am then in a position to judge those examples as less than my experience or more, automatically putting me in the space of duality. Do not judge your gifts; just embrace them, cherish them.

The transition of incorporating an experience of your life that you have previously labeled as painful and now view as positive is usually a process, even if it is an Aha! moment. Once you are able to process one event, you usually start to question more events in your life, and things can become overwhelming. Take your time. Be gentle with the process and yourself. I found it particularly difficult to comprehend that there really are not any wrong experiences until I began to view my life from a higher perspective and in an impersonal way; everything eventually brought me closer to my true self. Through this process of elimination, I was open to the gifts of the experience. As you know, and as I am sure you have experienced, the inner call to true fulfillment is beyond our control. Either we go with the flow of life calling unto itself with the help of Divine grace and acting on our Divine guidance, or we struggle upstream and exhaust ourselves by clinging to our illusions or frogs, trying desperately to make them into something they are not.

Seeing the Light in the Darkness

The separation from the Oneness or void we feel and experience is the result of falsely believing that we are separate from our Creator. We view ourselves as just one tiny sliver in the prism of the full spectrum of light. That is why our lives are never enough; we are looking for the completion of self in all the wrong places. We are looking outside ourselves instead of within, where the "prince" truly resides. Did the master Christ not tell us, "The kingdom is within"? Why do we insist on looking outside ourselves for it? We need foundational wisdom within us so we can build our lives and relationships on the awareness that we are already whole, and we are responsible for our peace, contentment, and happiness. Our connection to Oneness is the cake and all the other experiences of life are the frosting. That connection is based on the same principle as building a house on a solid foundation. We can build that foundation by undertaking the illuminating journey of discovering the Source of our souls.

Spirit is always calling us to our original Oneness, away from the illusion of separation and duality. You have heard the expression "It's all good." For years I had such distaste for that saying and for anyone who subscribed to it. I was convinced that anyone who would use that saying as a guiding principle in his or her life was unconscious and ignorant in believing such a thing. However, so-called truly bad encounters can be a means of pushing us to shift those of our beliefs that no longer serve our souls and that instead hold us back in our growth. Mawlana Jalal-al-Din Rumi, a thirteenth-century Persian poet and Sufi mystic, tells us that "the wound is the place where the Light enters you."

I do not make this statement lightly. I have spent more than twenty years of my life as a clinical nurse specialist in the HIV/AIDS arena, starting in 1989. During that time in the pandemic, our world was enveloped in the enormous grasp of fear of contracting the infection from casual contact. I have witnessed firsthand how devastating and cruel life can be. On a more personal note, my father abandoned me the day I came home from the hospital after birth. I was boarded out during my first year of life and later raised by a mostly absent alcoholic mother. I am also an incest survivor. I was orphaned by the time I was sixteen. These are just a few of the challenges I have encountered. I do not share those episodes in my life from a place of being a victim but rather to let you know that I know firsthand how events like these can empower you if you are willing to find the wisdom that lies in them.

After many, many years of searching for answers, I became open to the blessings of Divine grace, which allowed me to take in the teachings of amazing souls. I finally came to a place of true healing and wholeness. I can honestly say I would not want to change anything that happened to me because the challenges of my life delivered me to where I am today. That being said, I most definitely would like to change many of my reactions to those challenges. Since that is not possible, I have learned to forgive myself and strive to do better as I move forward.

To illustrate further this idea of "It's all good," I can tell you that many of my patients, especially in the beginning of the pandemic, knowing they were dying, told me that AIDS was one of the best things that had ever happened to them. They viewed this disease as the thing that stopped them from using illicit drugs or that ended a destructive lifestyle that had enmeshed them. Others shared with me that selling their bodies to get drugs was a horrific way to survive in this world. Others changed the way they looked at life and reconnected with estranged family members, knowing life was too short to hold a grudge, especially with the limited time they had left.

On a much lighter note, let us explore another way of becoming mindful that we are never alone. I am sure you have had the experience of receiving a thought that reminded you of something you were supposed to do. Your response has been, "Oh my God! How could I have forgotten to do that? I am so thankful that I remembered. It could have been a real disaster." I know that when this happened to me, I would think that I needed to make better lists of the things I needed to do, get more organized, and be more in control of my life. I admit I am a "control freak," as they say. So when I would forget something that I judged to be significant, I would beat up on myself. I decided to devise a better and more comprehensive plan so that "that" would never happen again. I am sure you already know where I am going with this. It is not possible to be in total control of our lives, or of much else, for that matter. Was it not one of the Beatles who said, "If you want to make God laugh, tell Him [or Her] your plans"?

I still believe we have a responsibility to engage in life in the most responsible way possible, to show up, and be fully present in our lives, and to hold ourselves accountable for our actions. However, I also have become aware that we are most certainly not alone in this arena. Countless times in my life (and again, I am sure, also in yours), a thought appears in my mind that alerts me to a danger or reminds me of what needed to be done or gives me a brilliant way of approaching a challenging task. Where do we think those thoughts come from? I now believe that we are receiving guidance through Divine grace all the time, but many times we are not allowing the space needed to receive those blessings. We get so caught up in our narrow vision of life that we forget the wisdom of "Be still and know that I am God."

Life flows more smoothly now that I know that I am surrounded by Divine grace. I have also found that the more I acknowledge and thank Spirit for the gifts of Divine grace and guidance, the more I receive and experience them. It is the same principle as keeping your cup turned up to collect the rain instead of letting the rain wash over the down-turned cup, or keeping the ember in touch with the flame to keep it burning, illuminating the dark. You can do this by staying connected to the flowing stream of Divine grace. As we become more and more aware of the presence of Spirit in our lives and acknowledge Spirit's presence, our connection to Spirit becomes stronger and stronger; we look to that connection as the first place to go for guidance rather than a last-ditch effort born of desperation.

HAVING AN INTIMATE RELATIONSHIP WITH GOD

In some aspects, your relationship with God is similar to other relationships you have. It needs to be nurtured and tended to continually: open communication and dedication, unconditional love and appreciation, and acceptance and trust are essential. Those ingredients may be described differently in your relationship with Spirit but are essentially the same: prayer, meaning open communication and dedication; devotion, meaning unconditional love and appreciation; and surrender, meaning acceptance and trust. Our own experience of the blessings Spirit bestows upon us will expand our acceptance and trust of what Spirit has to offer to support our spiritual growth. And like other relationships, it grows with time, and the bonds become resolute and more enduring.

The biggest difference in our relationship with Spirit is that we are always loved unconditionally. Many of us are incapable of truly comprehending how unconditional love is possible. For most of us, unconditional love conjures up thoughts of being a doormat or seems to be synonymous with being powerless, especially in our Western culture. Therefore it is beyond our understanding that Spirit loves each created being unconditionally and cherishes each one of us no matter what we have done.

We may attribute another component to Spirit: we may think that we are not capable of miracles. Many of us expect that Divine grace will appear in our lives like a bolt of lightning or that miracles happen just as dramatically. Little do we know that we can make such a dramatic difference in someone's life by doing something that we consider insignificant but that the other person may view as a miracle. How many times have you received Divine guidance disguised as a nudge or faint thought to phone or drop a line to someone, start a conversation with a total stranger, or smile to acknowledge someone you pass on the street? Inviting someone to a holiday meal who otherwise would have spent that holiday alone can feel like a miracle to that person. Even when we acknowledge these thoughts, these simple acts appear to be inconsequential to us, but the Divine grace that flows through us to the other may be exactly what that person needs at that exact moment in their lives. These simple actions may change the course of that person's life, yet we may never know it. This thought reminds me of the "peace prayer" of Saint Francis of Assisi that begins "O Lord, make me an instrument of your peace."

Where do these nudges come from, and what are they asking of us? The answer to this question goes back to what I expressed before. The Divine guidance we receive is a call from deep within to develop a relationship with that guidance and become more aware of the Divine grace that is always available to us. Divine grace is like the start of the early spring, its warmth melting the snow off the mountains, which begins with a trickle and eventually grows to a force that can carve canyons into mountains on the journey to the source of its beginning, the oneness of the ocean. Divine grace is a power that melts through our unconsciousness, beckoning us to become more and more aware of the Truth of who we are, the power that forges on to sculpt connections with an awareness of the Divine. As we grow in our trust of the Divine guidance we receive, we form an intimate bond with our inner world. Divine grace illuminates the journey to our inner world.

Caroline Myss, renowned spiritual teacher, scholar, medical intuitive, and best-selling author to whom I dedicate this book, refers to our inner world as the world behind our eyes versus the world in front of our eyes, our exterior world. When the world behind our eyes becomes more illuminated, we perceive the world in front of our eyes with a more conscious awareness. This shift in our perception creates a change in our external world as it follows a universal law, the law of cause and effect. The energetic vibration with which we come to view our exterior world is of a new vibrational frequency for us. As a result, the external world shifts to align with our new perception. We perceive the external world much differently than before.

For example, I am sure you have seen one of those graphic drawings with instructions to find a face in the picture of a tree. When we first look at the picture, all we see is the tree because it is something we are familiar with and expecting to see, but we do not see anything else. Because we have been told there was something else there, we try harder to see it, and sure enough, we see the face. Previously we were looking right at it but could not see it. After we have identified the face, it is easy to see the face every time we look at the picture. Our perception changed, and so the picture we were looking at the second time changed as well, the universal law of cause and effect in action.

I want to share an experience with you that I had more than thirty-five years ago that was very difficult for me to embrace at the time. In truth, it is still difficult for me to comprehend and incorporate my awareness into my consciousness. I was sitting outdoors enjoying a glorious afternoon as I was waiting for my children to get off the school bus. It was one of those days when the sky was breathtakingly blue and the majesty of the white cumulus clouds can make you feel thrilled to be alive. Being very present and witnessing this indescribable beauty, my mind turned to how truly awesome God's creation is. Suddenly, a "knowing," for lack of a better word, hit me like a ton of bricks. God could not be God without you because something would be missing from creation, and that is not possible in the Oneness. No matter how hard I tried to shake this from my awareness, the thought would not leave my mind. How could I possibly be that essential to God? I have the ability to grasp this intellectually at this stage in my life, but to this day I struggle in living my life in the constant consciousness of how very precious each and every aspect of creation is, especially when it comes to my importance to creation.

Words from chapter 64 of the *Tao Te Ching* may encourage you never to give up on the rigorous soul journey to know the Truth of who you are and how precious each and every sentient being is: "It is the single small step that begins the journey of a thousand miles."

I leave you in this chapter with a story that reminds me of how beautiful we are in the eyes of God, who sees us with different eyes than we see ourselves. This is a story about a beautiful Buddha image that was first located in Ayutthaya Siam in the thirteenth century. Several hundred years ago, the Burmese army was on the verge of invading Thailand, which at that time was called Siam. The Buddhist monks were very fearful that this Buddha image would be destroyed, so they took steps to camouflage the image. Fortunately, although all the monks were killed, the Buddha image was safe. In 1957 the monks at that time decided that the image should be moved to Bangkok. It was exceedingly heavy. Cranes were used to move it. In the process of moving the image, a crack in the clay of the image opened. This was of grave concern to the monks. The image was already outside the temple, and it was starting to rain, so the monks covered the image with tarps as best they could to prevent the clay from being destroyed.

During the night, one of the monks, concerned about what was happening to the image, went out in the dark to check on it. He carefully lifted the covering and shone his flashlight on it. Something odd happened: something was gleaming back at him. In the morning the monks examined the image and realized that there was indeed something under the clay. On further inspection they discovered that the image was made of gold. The monks, all those years ago, had covered the golden Buddha image in an eight-inch thick protective layer of clay to camouflage it in an effort to keep it safe from the Burmese army. None of those monks survived to tell of the beauty that was beneath the camouflage. This image is of a seated Buddha, ten feet tall, weighing more than five tons. It is believed to be nine hundred years old. It is now located at the Wat Tramit Temple of the Golden Buddha in Bangkok in all its radiance.

When I first heard this story, I thought of how similar our situation is to the story of the golden Buddha image. Over the years we have camouflaged ourselves in layers of false beliefs, material gain, titles, professional achievements, and the like. We seek to protect ourselves from the physical world, which some of us view as threatening if we do not get ahead and take care of ourselves, especially if we have been abandoned or betrayed by those we thought would protect us.

For those of you who are ready to open yourself to the Truth of who you are, reverently ask for Divine grace to wash away your false sense of security, your protective camouflage. Allow yourself to be vulnerable, call on the courage you have within your being, and humbly ask to have the precious golden being that you were created to be in the Oneness of the universe to be revealed to you: not for aggrandizement but for you to appreciate the gift of life that was freely given to you. The precious image beneath your camouflage, the Truth of who you are, is how you appear through the eyes of God, the Creator of you—a precious golden image.

In the next chapter we move into the realm of the mind and the ego. The sole function of the ego is to survive as a separate entity from the Oneness, which is impossible. The ego gets its energy for survival from the mind. An unconscious, unawakened mind supports the ego's survival by feeding on the illusions of the physical realm, which sustains the belief that we are separate and not interconnected. Again, we know Oneness experientially, not intellectually. We cannot reach Oneness by way of our intellect, reasoning mind, or our ego. The gift of the wisdom, the awareness of the Oneness of creation, that Divine Grace blesses us with will guide us through this maze of illusion.

Chapter 3

Illuminating Your Daily Life Through the Gift of Divine Grace:
The Third Eye Chakra

This amazing water overflows to purify our third eye chakra, and we understand it is washing away clouds of judgment and duality, allowing precious moments of clear vision. Saint Teresa of Avila described it as seeing God in the details of life from and with a mystical vision or perception.

What is usually condemned as "bad" by the mind and the mind-made self is actually grace coming into your life.
— *Eckhart Tolle*

All that we are is the result of what we have thought. The mind is everything. What we think we become.
— *Buddha*

THE THIRD EYE CHAKRA is associated with our rational, reasoning mind, which continually manufactures "nonreality" episodes of daily drama as we move through our lives. We are conditioned to separate the world in oppositional positions with our judgments. The very instant we judge something, we have automatically stepped out of the realm of Oneness and placed ourselves in duality, or in the terms of the Buddhist tradition, we have stepped into illusion. The veil of illusion creates a sense of separation from the Truth of who we are, one with the Oneness, and our egoic mind interprets the illusion as reality: this becomes our lives. Judgment positions everything into the world of polarities: dark and light, good and bad, right and wrong, negative and positive. The list goes on and on. I am sure you have seen the well-known Chinese symbol of yin yang, which represents a total balance of feminine and masculine energies. In the West most of us describe this symbol as yin and yang. By putting the "and" between the yin and the yang, we put those energies in opposition to each other, when, in reality, each gives rise to the other, which is contained in the other. Both are in perfect balance with each other. Illusion is similar to this. What appears as separate is really only the One beneath the veil of illusion. Our minds and our egos, the false sense of who we think we are that is attached to the mind, feeds on this false belief of separation, and we become unconsciously trapped in the illusion.

The Illusions of the Egoic Mind

Our consciousness was one with the Creator of the universe before we came into physical form. The circumstances we were born into began influencing that consciousness from day one of being in physical form. The culture we were born into, the traditions that surrounded us, as well as our individual direct experience of our physical environment have formed the consciousness that we now identify with. The totality of those interactions is the foundation of our perspective in relationship to our environment and the world around us today. Based on this appreciation of how our consciousness has developed and evolved because of our input, it is understandable that each of us has a much different view of what we call reality. Our surroundings are neutral; it is we who assign them the label of negative or positive. If you have done any traveling outside your immediate surroundings, you become aware of how different other people behave and view their environment. Traveling outside your country to other, distinctly different cultures really brings to light the differences between various perspectives of reality. For instance, a monsoon can be a dreaded event in one area, while in another, people are outside dancing in the rain and thankful that rain has finally arrived.

Everything in manifested form begins with thought, which in turn, creates the world we live in from our personal perspectives: The world according to *me*. Most of us get caught up unconsciously judging others based on our beliefs and the thoughts those beliefs generate. We may be drawn to strong, powerful people and admire them, while others' perspective of those same people may be one of arrogance and rudeness. "Beauty is in the eye of the beholder" is an axiom most of us are familiar with and certainly it rings true when we are exploring the realm of our world with a limited view of reality. Our fears and hopes are the filters we put on our perspective of reality. These innermost fears and hopes are a driving force in how we choose to interact with life because they lay the foundation for how we "show up" in life. This consumption of our being by illusion can cause us to inflict harm on our own lives and on all of manifested creation that we interact with. You can pray to see the world around you through the eyes of Creator, the eyes of Oneness. Saint Teresa of Avila told us to see God in the details of our day. I add to that: experience God in the details of our day.

Jean Houston is a scholar, philosopher, prolific author, and consultant to the United Nations. She has a similar belief as expressed by Eckhart Tolle in the quotation at the beginning of this chapter, that great difficulty in our lives can be an opportunity to delve deep within our souls to discover the potential life-changing wisdom that the wounding contains. Our perspective of negative events that have occurred or are occurring in our lives has the power to create a victim mentality within us, distorting our reality. Alternatively, these events can create the motivation to uncover the gems of wisdom these events hold, revealing a deeper understanding of our soul.

Charles J. Givens, a financial adviser and motivator, had a very difficult childhood. Those childhood experiences brought him the realization that he was the one to determine his future life. His belief is similar to many teachers in that your only real power in this universe is the "now." He points out that we are where we are, but where we are going is up to us. His words contain profound wisdom. We have the power to choose our destinies; the choice is up to us. Even in dire circumstances, some have chosen the path of light instead of the dark.

Building on the premise that we have the power to choose our reality, I would like to share a simple story I heard many years ago when I was studying Eastern beliefs. It illustrates the concept of illusion, what in the Hindu tradition is called *maya*. The word *maya* means "not that" and is taken from the Sanskrit root words *ma,* meaning "that" and *ya,* meaning "not." Knowing that we have the power to create our reality, we can see how easily it is to get caught up in the fear of our negative perspectives.

A young boy is walking down a dark path at night all alone to return to his village. The noises of the night add to his distress. He becomes more and more fearful of the dark as he continues on his journey to his destination. His eyes are focused on the path in front of him, but his mind is consumed with foreboding. In the dim light of the moon, he catches a glimpse of something on the path ahead of him but cannot clearly make it out. Intuitively he slows his pace. As he gets slightly closer to this object, he is stricken by panic: he can see a snake lying in the middle of the path trying to absorb the last of the warmth of the hot day. His heart races faster, and his breathing becomes even more shallow and rapid. He frantically tries to figure out how he can get by this snake and make his way safely home. After a fearful assessment of this terrifying predicament, he concludes that there does not seem to be an alternative route around this snake.

The boy summons all the courage available to him at the time and ever so cautiously and quietly creeps closer and closer to the source of his fear in the hope that he can tiptoe by the snake by stepping along the edge of the path. As he gets almost next to the snake, he realizes that this fear-provoking snake is simply a piece of discarded rope lying on the path. The rope, which was the initiator of the boy's panic, did not change; it was simply the boy's perception of the rope that changed.

This story is an excellent example of how our perspective is the basis of how we create our world. Our minds create our thoughts, which in turn dictate our perspective of the world we live in. These thoughts are based on the conscious and unconscious beliefs we have incorporated into our perspective of what we call reality. The mind is capable of creating such powerful illusions, crippling us from progressing on our soul's journey of illumination when we are caught in the drama of illusion, in the *maya*. We tend to react to life, the situation at hand, instead of going within, asking for Divine guidance to help us discern what our response to an incident should be. When we are conscious that we are one with the Oneness of God, we can connect with that Source, seeking the guidance that will illuminate the illusion so we can release ourselves from the power of our mind's illusions, just as the boy's fear was released when he became aware that the threatening snake was only a non-threatening rope.

It appears that the power of our minds has the ability to create an experience even when we leave our physical bodies in a near-death experience. Elisabeth Kübler-Ross, M.D., a psychiatrist who did ground-breaking research on near-death experiences and was a best-selling author, shares the results of her research, which supports the belief that we create what we believe. The title of one of her most well known books is *On Death and Dying,* in which she describes the stages of dying. This work established what is now known as the Kübler-Ross model. Her research in near-death experiences included interviews with thousands of people who experienced a near-death event, resulting in her conclusion that most people's deaths were what they thought they would be. For instance, if the person believed that he or she would see friends or family members who had died before them, that is what they experienced. If the person believed death would be a peaceful experience, it was. If they believed a religious figure would greet them, they did. Kübler-Ross's research substantiates the concept that what we believe becomes our reality, even in near-death experiences.

She encourages us to get in touch with the stillness within our being and to become aware that all that happens in life are blessings that are given for us to learn from and that there are no coincidences or mistakes. I found her belief to be in alignment with my belief of going within to find the Truth and then create our world from the wisdom we are given.

Our minds' perspectives strongly influence our judgments, which can be rigidly black or white, contain shades of gray, or allow for a full spectrum of color. Bernard Haisch, the astrophysicist I wrote about in chapter two, described how optical filters determine the colors in the picture we see projected on the screen we are viewing. Similarly, we view our lives through our individual and tribal filters and beliefs (I explore this in depth in chapter eight.) Life experiences certainly contribute to the filters we adopt to adjust our perspective of life and consequently mold our beliefs and influence how we interact with our world. For the most part, we act in ways that are in alignment with our concept of ourselves, directing how we interact with our world, whether we are conscious of this behavior or not. Our concepts, and consequently our actions, shift as our beliefs shift. Beliefs are simply the result of habitual thoughts. However, we have the ability to shift the focus of our minds and thoughts, which will result in shifts in our beliefs. When we gain the ability to shift our beliefs, our lives will take a decidedly different path. This is in alignment with Buddha's quote: "All that we are is the result of what we have thought. The mind is everything."

We need to involve ourselves in activities that quiet our minds and bring us closer to the Truth of who we are, such as meditation, prayer, contemplation, being in nature, listening to music that inspires us, looking at majestic art, or getting into the zone of a runner's high. Anything that brings us to a place of stillness in our minds will shift our energy to a frequency that is more aligned with the essence of Spirit, and our thoughts will therefore also align with that vibrational frequency. To assist in this endeavor, we can always humbly ask for Divine grace to illuminate the illusionary beliefs of our lives that no longer serve our souls and therefore our greater good.

There are numerous activities that are similar to the ones I have mentioned that will quiet the mind. The list would be too extensive to include here. Suffice it to say, the more time we spend in a peaceful state of mind, aligned with the essence of Spirit, the more we will naturally gravitate away from thoughts that are unsettling since stillness is our true nature. We will develop less tolerance for periods of unrest within. The awareness that we are never separated from Oneness will become the basis of our consciousness as we progress on our soul's journey. Again, it is indeed rare for a person to remain in this awareness of Oneness; however, the more we align and experience this Truth, the more it becomes the basis of our belief system.

My experience is that by surrounding myself with people whose priority is to focus on the illumination of their soul's journey, reading sacred mystical works, having a disciplined meditation and prayerful spiritual practice, spending time in devotion, reflection, and contemplation results in a significant effect on shifting my thoughts and subsequently my beliefs to a more spiritually attuned nature. I once spent a week with a Yaqui shaman, Lench Archuleta, in the Arizona desert, and he continually reminded me that when I changed, everything around me would change. I have found this to be true in my life. Again Buddha's quote rings true. I can honestly say that I am amazed at how dramatically my life changes as I shift my thought process. Many of the beliefs that dominated and con-trolled my life for far too many decades as a result of being trapped by my mind have dissipated.

THE MONKEY MIND

I love the story of the Monkey Mind. This is another concept I came across in my studies of Eastern beliefs that further illustrates being trapped by the power of our mind. This simple story reaffirms the principle that our minds create powerful illusions. In India, as in many other countries, there are families of monkeys that roam around villages at will. They steal any object that catches their attention, especially food that is unattended. Some villagers will place a banana in a very large jar with a small neck and leave it unattended in a place that the monkey will be sure to encounter it. The monkey finds the jar, inserts its hand, and grabs the banana. The monkey cannot retrieve the banana from the jar, however, because the opening of the neck of the jar is too small to accommodate the monkey's clenched fist. The monkey, thinking it is trapped, is now easier to catch because of the impediment of this large jar it is attached to —emphasis on *attached.* No matter how hard the monkey tries to shake itself free, it is of no use; it is still trapped. All the monkey needs to do is simply open its hand and easily slip it out of the trap to freedom, but it clings to the banana for dear life, putting its freedom in great jeopardy, all because of the illusion of being trapped.

Now take another simple example, one that most of us have experienced, to demonstrate further the principle of polarity and duality as an illusion. Think of a food you have *hated* as a child. Hatred is a pretty rigid judgment and is clearly aligned with the negative aspect of that food. It might have been the actual taste or consistency of the food, someone else's opinion, or an emotional connection. As you grew up, let us suppose that you "acquired a taste" for the food and it is now one of your favorites and aligned with the positive aspect of this food. What changed? There could be some differences in the food itself. Maybe you bought it fresh and cooked it yourself, whereas before it was presented to you cooked from the frozen form, though essentially, it is the same food. Obviously, the thing that changed was your mind's judgment of the food. We can use this extremely simple, unemotionally charged example to help us understand the power our minds have over our beliefs and actions and therefore our lives.

I hope I have given you a glimpse of the possibility of how your perspective of yourself may be trapped in previous life events. The mind is a powerful tool, one that can guide us on the journey of our souls when it is not consumed with illusions. However, the enormous delusional power that our minds contain to incapacitate us from living our lives as we were truly created to live is undisputable. Our conscious beliefs and, what is more unnerving, our unconscious beliefs and fears, can distort our understanding of almost anything.

Another power is beyond our minds, one that we can always call on when we believe we are ensnared by the complexities that life presents and we are unable to use our minds to release ourselves from it. That power is the power of Divine grace that can illuminate the predicament we find ourselves in by lifting the veil of illusion our minds have created. Be "in" stillness, and reverently open yourself to receive the blessing of Divine grace. By developing a disciplined spiritual practice, we establish a foundation of connectedness to the Truth of who we are, and that foundation will prevail in our consciousness, assisting us in times of uncertainty, fear, and confusion. We become aware of when we are out of alignment with our inner being in a timelier manner and are able to still our minds and ask for Divine grace and guidance to illuminate the plight we find ourselves in.

TRAPPED BY THE MONKEY MIND

GOING WITHIN: Let us explore examples of significant events that you can identify from your own life that will shed light on the beliefs you have had and the changes in your life that occurred when those beliefs shifted. Then we will move into exploring current beliefs that reflect the principle of duality and illusion in your life today. I am sure you can come up with examples of things in your life about which you have changed your perspective, relationships, family traditions, or cultural or ethnic beliefs.

Think of a belief that you were always absolutely sure was true. As you moved on in your life, that belief changed. If, at the time you held that belief, someone had tried to tell you that one day you would change your mind regarding it, do you think you would have been open to that comment, or would you have known beyond a shadow of a doubt that you were right and your opinion would never change? "Never" and "always" can be limiting concepts and can hold us prisoner to beliefs and positions that no longer serve our souls.

Reflect deeply on instances in your life when your judgment shifted as you became aware that a tightly held yet ill-serving belief was not true. If you can cite even a few examples from your life, not a concept you heard or read about, but a belief in your own life that illustrates a time when you were lost in an illusion, you are well on your way to understanding the daunting challenge of being trapped in illusion. Please pause here to contemplate at least one change you have made in your thoughts, something significant that occurred in your life that resulted in a shift in your belief and therefore a change in your life. Take time for yourself to write your experience or experiences in your journal, knowing that the act of writing will help you to focus your thoughts and will bring your nonphysical thoughts into the physical realm by being recorded on paper. The process of documenting the change in your perspective may provide you with a deeper perception of how the experience may have influenced other aspects of your life.

Hopefully, you were able to reflect on at least one change you have made in your life once you were able to release yourself from the illusion your mind had created. This reflection will ground your awareness that you are capable of dissolving a belief that had kept you from being aligned with your soul because it is an experience from your *own* life that is indisputable.

Shift now to your present life circumstances. Remembering the story of the Monkey Mind and the monkey's clenched fist, quiet your mind and reflect on at least one belief or perspective you intuitively know does not serve you anymore, although you cannot release it, for whatever reason. The reason in many situations is fear of change. You intuitively know that if you give up this belief it will shift that aspect of your life and your life will undoubtedly change. What is the "banana" that you been unable to let go of that keeps you trapped? Are you currently ruminating over a perceived problem that plagues you? Are you afraid of being judged or disowned by friends or family if you were to release a traditional belief that no longer serves you? Are you afraid that you will be humiliated because you have admitted the belief was wrong? Sincerely and prayerfully, humbly ask for Divine grace to shed light on this perceived challenge so that the gift of knowledge and wisdom that it contains will be revealed to you. Open yourself to Divine grace and guidance, which will give you insight on how to release the impediment that is hampering your soul's journey on its path of illumination. Remind yourself of the previous reflection, when you had already been successful in releasing a belief and the freeing results that ensued.

Your acknowledgment of how you were limited in an area of your life before you shifted your perspective will give you confidence and encouragement. You will be able to release constrictions that are ingrained in the belief system you have created in your mind. Whether you are conscious or unconscious of them, Divine grace will reveal the gift those constrictions offer. Take time to write down the belief that has you in bondage; this time, write about why the belief is so hard to release. Be sure to include the new wisdom that was revealed to you. As often as needed, repeat this reflection with other beliefs that have a hold on you and that you are struggling with. Reflect on your writings periodically to remind yourself of the newly revealed wisdom that you were blessed with and how your life has shifted as a result.

~

Not long ago, an event took place in my life that left upheaval in its wake. I was too blinded by my version of the event to see what was really happening. At the time of the event I was working as a clinical nurse supervisor for sixteen employees, including social workers and nurses. I was training a fairly new social worker who appeared to be challenged by her job responsibilities. She came to me to relate a difficult situation she was having with one of her co-workers, a nurse who shared patients with this social worker.

During my meeting with her to discuss the situation, she allowed herself to become vulnerable and explained that she had always run from situations of confrontation, like the one she was describing. Under the disguise of what I would characterize as "I'm not going to put up with this," otherwise known as fear, she would leave her job. She stated that she wanted to move beyond her usual course of action and handle the situation more professionally. She related that she really loved the work she was doing and wanted to resolve the friction between her and her co-worker before it escalated beyond the point that she felt she would need to leave her job. What she was experiencing was her growing new awareness of the potential to stop herself from her reactionary behavior, based in her unconscious reaction to fear. In an effort to help me understand why she usually fled from these types of situations, she described a challenging childhood and an adult life that was just as difficult. She had a deep belief in God, which she was able to share with anyone. We spent a great deal of time together discussing ways to approach the situation she found herself in with her colleague, and we agreed upon a plan she was comfortable with.

That plan would allow her to express her concerns in a safe and supportive environment in a nonthreatening, nonconfrontational way about her relationship with the nurse and the effect the situation was having on patients they shared. I was to meet with the nurse first to allow her to share her perspective of the situation. We would then all meet together. Our group meeting went exceptionally well. Both parties ended the meeting by sharing their mutual appreciation; they even hugged before parting.

The social worker meeting the challenges of her job responsibilities was not resolved quite so easily, however. She continued to fall behind in her work and needed frequent reminders on how to perform her responsibilities. My concern grew over how her deficiencies affected her patients. I had been flexible in judging her job performance because I was aware of the challenges she faced and because her connection to Spirit strongly resonated with me. Yet it became apparent that patient services were being affected. I needed to address the social worker's inability to keep her records in compliance with our agency's contract with a federally funded program. Once again, I reviewed her patient records and found that things were worse than I anticipated, despite all the supervision and encouragement she had been given. One of her patients had not been contacted in months. That event was really the final thing that made me realize that my personal connection to her needed to be put aside. I informed her by voicemail that we needed to formalize a written plan to address her performance since the oral plan she had agreed to had not resulted in the accomplishment of her stated goal.

Here is how the illusions of this situation played out. The social worker perceived my voicemail message as a firing; she cleaned out her personal belongings that day and then requested a meeting with the program director and me. During our meeting she asked the director to listen to my voicemail. The director had listened to it and reported that the social worker must have misunderstood my message, as she had not been "fired." The social worker then accused me of having fabricated the facts of her performance. I suggested that the three of us look at her patient records.

It was quite a distance to the site, so I had plenty of time to build my case about her performance, fueled by my integrity having been questioned. I went directly to the record that showed she had not attempted to contact a patient for months. The documentation was there for all to see. I gathered more records for us to review together. Regarding the record that showed there

79

had not been contact for months, the social worker asked me to look further back into the notes as they would show that she had contacted the patient. Much to my surprise, misfiled notes confirmed her statement about this one particular patient. I had been too consumed with pride to see the illusion clearly. Instead, I had focused on the medical standard that the most recent patient information be filed appropriately. She had hit on one of my most vulnerable beliefs, and I could not let go of my anger at her even questioning my integrity. I was trapped. Needless to say, the lengthy review of her other patient files did not go well. My Achilles heel had been exposed. All that followed had therefore been motivated by my personal weakness. The program director was uncomfortable. Anyone who was later involved in this situation also became uncomfortable. This drama was difficult for all the players.

In that moment, I did not recognize the gift that the experience offered. I reverted to my basic instincts, the emotion of anger engaged the arrogant shadow component of my being. There was no turning back at that point. I became lost in the illusion that I needed to prove that I was beyond falsifying facts and that I was right.

As I prayed and reflected on the event for days, my awareness grew of just how out of alignment I had been in the encounter. Intuitively, I knew that the experience was one that would reveal wisdom for my life if I could go beyond my mind and my need to be right. I searched my soul with an intense desire to uncover how I had gotten so out of alignment from my strong belief in compassion and unconditional love. With a great deal of soul searching and meditation I realized that my Monkey Mind would not release my perspective of an attack on my integrity. This obsession clouded my vision and my actions entirely. My pride had controlled how I reacted impulsively in the moment, and I was left defenseless against my anger and indignation. This inner search made me realize that the social worker was the *noble adversary* that Buddha had described in his teachings. A *noble adversary* is someone who is a teacher in your life, not in a formal sense, but someone who can precipitate an intense journey deep within your soul, searching for the Truth of the situation you find yourself in.

Once I was able to regain my center, I was able to view the event with detachment. I felt great compassion for the social worker because we had faced many similar childhood challenges. I truly admired her strength and her willingness to share her sense of vulnerability and fear in the situation with her co-worker. I knew she had a deep relationship with God, and I admired her for her convictions. My connection to her created the perfect scenario. I was caught off guard by her accusations and my vulnerability, the ego-centered pride I had in my sense of unquestionable integrity, took over.

I became grateful and appreciative of the experience, after a great deal of "going within," and was able to retrieve the nugget of gold out of the cauldron of molten lead my anger had produced in the situation. Consequently, I was able to interact with this person in an unconditionally loving and compassionate manner in subsequent encounters. The issue of her not performing her job responsibilities was the vehicle that showed me how my pride in my integrity and ability to carry out my job responsibilities had blinded me. I had entered the encounter with all those involved from a place of anger rather than a place of what was really going on. My being right and proving it were my priorities at the time.

This synchronistic event brought us together in perfect timing and tone. It was an affirmation of my belief that unconditional love and forgiveness do conquer fear and resentment. When I came to peace within myself and was able to appreciate the wisdom the illusion contained, I was able to thank the social worker in person for the priceless awareness she brought into my life. She was able to share with me that she appreciated the opportunity to thank me for what she had been able to learn from the experience. As in the meeting she had with her coworker, we hugged and expressed our feelings for each other. It appeared that once we each gained the wisdom of the situation, our need to interact dissolved, as some time later she left her position quite unexpectedly.

This event, like so many others in my life, reminds me of the "knowing" that you cannot make this stuff up, even if you wanted to. Too many things had to come together for this play to unfold to be just a coincidence. I was left with confirmation of my conviction that we are always being cared for and surrounded by Divine grace, even when we and others are caught up in the wake of upheaval from circumstances we ourselves have created.

GOING WITHIN: If this example of a *noble adversary*, a person who takes you deep within your shadow, strikes a chord with something that has happened in your own life, take time to reflect on your own experience. Feel the emotion and energy of the event that your perspective colored as a threatening situation, so much so that you allowed yourself to be pulled into that illusion and made yourself vulnerable to your shadow energy. Take advantage of that life experience as a way to assist you out of that illusion, into the revelation of your vulnerabilities that still affect your life today and the wisdom that experience holds. Ask for and be open to the power of Divine grace that surrounds you with peace and comfort as you release the fear and judgment that you have been carrying with you. Create the space in your soul to receive the revelation of the wisdom the situation held. Embrace and honor the wisdom you have received because you were willing to be open to seeing the Truth of this life event. Stay there in that sacred place of revelation and bask in its unconditional love and peace for as long as you need to. Integrate the experience of connecting with Divine grace and the wisdom it revealed into your life experience. Draw from this firsthand experience of revelation, knowing you can always come here again when life challenges your beliefs and you need a refuge to go deep within.

≈

Know that what you receive in this sacred place will not only change the quality of your life but will also affect those you come in contact with: "When I change, all things change." Be sure to write in your journal about the event and the wisdom that was revealed to you. Trust me, if you are anything like me, your notes will come in very handy for the next illusion and out-of-alignment event in your life. I wish I could tell you that once you gain clarity on one situation you are home free on that issue. At least for me, it has not worked that way. However, I have found that without as much struggle, I am able to reach the core of the illusion by recognizing that whatever issue I am dealing with, it really is all about me and my perspective, and not that of the other person. I am also able to align with my center of compassion and unconditional love much sooner, for which I am most grateful.

RETRIEVING YOUR SPIRIT

You may come to appreciate duality for the teacher it is. When you become aware that you are feeling agitated or catch yourself ruminating over an incident you have had with someone, go within to find a way to view the incident from a higher perspective. Try to determine what the illusion is that you have attached yourself to. Relationships with other people, even very casual ones, are the best teachers of how we become attached to an illusion, primarily because relationships are connected to our emotions. When you can hold on to the awareness that the power struggle you are involved in is about you and not attempt to shift the blame to others for your inability to hold your center, you are more capable of recognizing the struggle as a teaching moment. This is an example of being empowered instead of being a victim. There is a saying that when we blame someone else for our disharmony, our blame (be-lame) reduces us to victim status because we have given over our power to the illusion, and consequently, to the other person.

Whatever word or words you use to describe the world you think your world is, consciously take this perspective to the world within, beyond the limits of your mind, to the realm of your soul. In this sacred place, you move beyond that description and open to expansiveness and inspiration. You, beyond your narrow intellect and perspectives, are governed by your "soul knowledge" when you open yourself to its power. When you become conscious that you have been touched by Divine grace and wisdom, you open yourself to experiencing the alluring world of illumination, moving out of the trappings of the physical world and its illusions into the world of vision and Truth. You become like a child, innocent, open to the wonderment of the world you now perceive instead of being trapped by your reasoning mind and the illusions it creates. You live more and more in the present moment, not losing your essence to the guilt and regret of your past and beyond the fear of the "what ifs" of the future.

Remember that for most of us the path of illumination is a long process, not something we can put into practice consistently the way an enlightened being can. Do not be discouraged or think yourself a failure if you are not able to become enlightened. Be thankful for the illumination you already have. Read about the lives of the mystics and sages. It does not matter what tradition they are from; they struggled on their path as well. The sharing of their attempts will be comforting to your own unfolding. People who are regarded in high esteem, like Mahatma Gandhi and Mother Teresa, openly shared their shortcomings. Neither of these great souls gave up on themselves. They reverently continued on their soul's journey, humbly seeking Divine grace and guidance along the way to alignment with the Source within them. They earnestly searched for aspects of their being that continued to become attached to illusions in the realm of duality in which they lived. Souls that are drawn to this path leave no stone unturned on the journey of illumination, for they have tasted the sweetness of connection to Spirit and nothing is worth the price of losing that connection.

Let us now explore a belief that you were taught by mostly well meaning people because it was the belief that they had been taught and continue to believe. The one I would like to explore with you is the belief that we are separate from what we know as God, Creator, Spirit, or Source. Please approach this reflection that explores your spiritual tradition respectfully. If you are in a place in your life that you are supported by the spiritual tradition that you were taught as a child, please skip this reflection.

Most of us, especially in the West, have been taught, in one way or another, that the entity known fairly universally as God is somewhere outside ourselves. The term most of us are familiar with for that place is *heaven*. Many of us were taught songs, prayers, and stories as children that refer to the entity as being "up there." On some occasions we even lift our eyes upward or make a hand gesture toward heaven when discussing the entity. Our teaching tends to involve asking the entity for things we want for others or ourselves. When what we ask for does not materialize, we may think we are not good enough to receive it, that there must be something wrong with us, that our prayers are not of the right composition, or our petitions have not been heard. I was trained in the Roman Catholic tradition as a child and remember being told that a difficult situation might be "my cross to bear" in life or that I should "offer my suffering up to God." Somehow I never remember being told as a child that the place to look for insight into an onerous situation was within, or that I should commune with my soul and ask for the Divine grace of illumination from the Source who created me for assistance.

This reflection is not about blaming your tradition for the harm you may have felt was done to you or for the difficulty you feel it created in your life. Because of the illusions that entangled them, our religious teachers may not have been aware of how Spirit is present in every aspect of our lives. At this point in my soul journey, I am convinced Spirit is always closer to us than is our very breath. Spirit is our constant companion and comforter. Another example from my life may clarify the essence of what I am trying to help you discover, that we are never alone or separated from our Source.

During a time of crisis in my life, I enrolled in a class given by Caroline Myss that comprised three long weekends over the course of a year. One of the first homework assignments was to go on a search to discover where we had left pieces of souls — not in a physical location but an ethereal location — those pieces of our soul that were still trapped in our pasts, preventing us from being present in our lives now. She explained that when we could discover where we had left those pieces and retrieve them, we could be more present in our lives and therefore more empowered.

At that time on my soul's journey I referred to myself as a recovering Catholic. For those of you who are not familiar with the term *recovering* in regard to overcoming a profoundly negative issue in your life, think of it in terms of recovering from alcohol or drug addiction. I had not been a practicing Catholic for more than thirty years but still dealt with many issues of "fear-based principles" relevant to God that I had been taught as a child, such as being unworthy, the existence of hell, and eternal damnation. Those teachings had an intensely negative effect on my life; I knew intuitively that I needed to heal that effect at a deeper level than I had before.

One day, after returning from my first class, I was on my way to a business meeting in another area of my state. I drove by the Roman Catholic church and adjacent school I had attended, where I had made my first communion and attended kindergarten and grade school. The door to the church was open, but no activity, such as a funeral or a mass, seemed to be taking place. It was unusual for the door to be open when no one was attending the church. I found myself thinking of my homework assignment (I doubt this was a coincidence). I decided that if I found the church door open on my way back from my meeting, I would go inside in an attempt to retrieve a portion of my soul that I perceived had been taken from me. Sure enough, the door was open when I was heading back to my office, and still there did not seem to be any activity. I parked my car and went in through the back door. A man was there doing minor repair work, which may have explained why the door was open.

I knelt at the altar and lighted a candle. Then I knelt in a pew, as I had done so many times before in that church. I reverently prayed and openly waited quite some time for a message or insight but received none. I left the church, and a knowing came that I should go to the adjoining parking lot, which was the playground of the school I had attended. Again I prayed and asked for insight and again received nothing. I gave up and walked back to my car feeling fairly dejected that the adventure had been uneventful.

As I was complaining in my mind of my disappointment, a block of thought came all at once. It was something like this: The fear of hell that I had held on to had in fact kept me safe when I was sixteen and my single mother was hospitalized for months before she died. I lived essentially alone for months and had plenty of opportunity to get into trouble during that period, involving drinking, drugs, sex, and the like. I was a rebellious adolescent, as most adolescents are, but I was also a definite risk taker. It was truly the fear of God and hell that kept me from becoming involved in dangerous activities. I could feel distinctly the energy of anger and guilt release and a sense of wonderment and comfort fill me. Even though for decades I no longer feared God or believed in hell, the experience filled me with the knowing that I had always been looked after, no matter how negative

I had perceived life to be. As I reflect on many moments of my life, I become aware of how many times I was surrounded by Divine grace but was unaware. The Yaqui shaman I wrote of before had another teaching he repeated frequently: "Thing are never what they appear to be." For me, the fear I had blamed on the church for years was certainly an example of that teaching in this revelation.

GOING WITHIN: Deeply reflect on the teachings you received on the nature of God in your childhood, or however the Source of creation was referred to in your tradition. Ask yourself how those teachings have influenced your life to this day. Even if you have not been conscious of how those teachings have affected you, positively or negatively, reflect on how those beliefs have and continue to express themselves in your life experience. Reverently ask what deep impact the spiritual teachings have had on your life and for the illumination of any illusions you have created about them as a result. Prayerfully ask for the power of Divine grace to reveal to you the wisdom of how the beliefs have affected your decisions along the way of your soul's journey. Open yourself to the answers. After spending time within your being, write about the insights you received about the beliefs and any new awareness and wisdom you receive.

Were you given new insights or expanded awareness of your concept of Spirit? If so, how will you incorporate the new awareness into your daily interactions of life? Can you develop a plan that will support a way for you to remember the insights? Treat the new awareness as you would a seedling. Feed your new awareness with thoughts that fill your soul with light and love, water it with your cleansed awareness, and protect the new understanding of your connection to the One. Surround yourself with like-minded souls to help you firmly root the revelations in your consciousness. Hold these gifts of wisdom close to your heart until the tentacles of the gift permeate your awareness and become an intricate part of your belief system. Be sure to record the new revelations in your journal.

Eckhart Tolle's quote at the beginning of this chapter speaks to the potential that loss can have in our lives as an awakener when we do not run from it. He informs us that the mind's perspective of loss is bad, but that loss can be Divine grace coming into our lives. For this reflection, the subject matter that you will explore can be in the realm of physical or nonphysical losses.

GOING WITHIN: Quiet your mind and go within to connect with your concept of loss. Spend some time here contemplating the subject of loss and what your beliefs are regarding loss. Do you still carry the feelings of a particular loss with you today? Identify what your feelings were that were connected to the experience. Write about at least one experience in your life, or more if you choose, when you lost something or someone that you were significantly attached to. Include your beliefs and feelings about that loss that come to your mind in present time. After you complete writing in your journal, read the following haiku by Mizuta Masohide, a seventh-century Japanese poet:

Barn's burnt down —
Now
I can see the moon.

Reflect on the haiku, take it within, and sit with it for a few minutes. Feel the message it has to offer you. Notice your reaction and the tone of your emotion in your reaction to it. Ask for Divine grace to illuminate the wisdom of the haiku so that you may claim that wisdom for your own. Has your reaction to it created an opening for a new insight to the loss you were reflecting on, or to loss as a whole? Was a space created for a different belief to emerge into your awareness that will change the way you perceive this loss and losses in the future? Be sure to write about the insights you received, capturing this new wisdom for future use when you experience loss, as inevitably you will.

MIRACLES DO HAPPEN

Can you expand your mind to the place where miracles are real? *A Course in Miracles* states, "miracles are examples of right thinking, aligning your perception with truth as God ordered it." Albert Einstein told us that we might live our lives as though nothing is a miracle or think that everything is a miracle. He told us that the choice was ours. These words of wisdom certainly affirm that with God, all things are possible, something to keep in mind when we are struggling with the illusions that trap us.

We must go beyond the limitations of our reasoning mind and our ego belief that we are separate from the One. It is a belief that roots us in the illusion of duality in our world. Recall those past obstacles in your life that your perspective created and how your perspective created those obstacles. Then recall the revelations you received that transformed your perspective into a different and, one hopes, liberating new belief and awareness. Remind yourself when you remain trapped in a situation of the familiar saying: "This too shall pass," but with a new understanding. Now, you are not referring to the "time" you will need for it to pass, but rather to the shifting of your awareness that it is your *attachment* to your perspective of the situation that will release you from its hold. On the lighter side of looking at illusion, Mark Twain told us, "I have suffered very many things in my life. Most of them never happened."

In Korean Zen, a branch of Buddhism, there is a teaching known as Don't Know Mind. My understanding of this teaching is that when we are able to release our limited, fixed perspectives and judgments, we liberate ourselves from the bondage of our narrow minds. Think of your mind like your email inbox. When your mind is full, there is no room for the messages Spirit wants to send you. We need to go through the messages carefully and hit delete for those that no longer serve our souls, creating the space to receive Spirit's insights and revelations. Socrates said that an unexamined life is not worth living. It has been reported that when he was told that he was the wisest man, he responded that it was probably true, for he knew enough to know that he knew nothing.

As we leave this chapter, focusing on the mind and illusion, I hope you were able to release beliefs that no longer serve your soul and that have weighed you down with baggage that keeps you from being able to be present in your life today, separating you from the Oneness of the universe. Remember the quote from Buddha at the beginning of the chapter, "What we think, we become." Are you ready to let go of what you think you know to be true for what you can and will know to be true when you trust in the Divine? Joseph Campbell said, "We must be willing to get rid of the life we have planned so as to have the life that is waiting for us." Your new insights and wisdom, illuminated by Divine grace, will serve you in ways that will nurture your soul as you move toward "the life that is waiting for you."

The next step is to allow the insights and wisdom that were revealed in your reflections to flow into your will, the power that dictates the choices you make in all your thoughts, words, and deeds, which we will explore in the next chapter.

CHAPTER 4

MELTING THE RESISTANCE OF YOUR WILL BY THE POWER OF DIVINE GRACE:

THE THROAT CHAKRA

Divine grace directs this pure stream of water to flow into our throat chakra and begins to clear away the constrictions of our narrow will and perspective. We begin to become aware of an energy that is building pressure behind this resistance of our beliefs and egotistical ways of trying to control our world according to our standards.

> The greatest distance on earth is the distance between the head and the heart.
> —*Anonymous*

> Most folks are as happy as they make their minds to be.
> —*Abraham Lincoln*

IN THIS CHAPTER WE EXAMINE your will and your power of choice. Your choices in thought, word, and deed affect every aspect of your life. Abraham Lincoln's words reflect that truth; however, not only do we choose to believe whether we will be happy, we get to make choices about most things in our lives. Those choices have their roots in the beliefs we base our lives on. It is said that love is the most powerful force we have. However, as Caroline Myss points out, we *choose* to love unconditionally or conditionally. So is it love or our choices that contain the most power in our lives?

Some of our choices are based on our conscious beliefs. However, many, many of our beliefs are unconscious, habitual patterns that are instinctual or were taught to us as we grew up. Some of those beliefs were taught orally and non-orally and are the platform from which we make our choices to this day. We are all aware at one or another level of the effect our surroundings have had on us. You can use the revelations of your reflections to probe the choices you make, what beliefs those choices are based on, and their effect on your journey of self-empowerment and illumination of your soul.

Now that you are able to be aware of the connection that Divine grace has had to the life experiences you have reflected on, my hope is that you will no longer be able to deny that Divine grace has been and is a constant presence in your life. If that is the case, you are now beyond the point of being unaware that Divine grace is a powerful component of how the events in your life are unfolding, even if you are completely unaware of its presence at the time. With these new revelations of Divine grace's presence in your life under your belt, if you will, let us move on to another aspect of aligning with the Truth of who you are.

Did you give much thought to the anonymous quote of this chapter; "The greatest distance on earth is from the head to the heart?" What was your immediate response to it? Did you think it could be an accurate reflection of your own life? Did it resonate with you and make you think of what impediments might lie on the path between your head and your heart? Let us delve into the content of the power of the throat chakra, your will, and the center of choice that lies between your head and your heart, exploring why it is essential to discover how this power center is connected to the quotation and to your soul's journey.

THE POWER OF YOUR WILL

In the previous chapter on the third eye chakra, we explored how illusions can be pervasive in our thoughts and minds and consequentially have an enormous impact on our lives and indeed create a particular reality. Your will, which is the power that creates your choices, is the deciding force as to which of your beliefs make it to your heart center. We will return to the deep inner dwelling of your true being that will allow you to discover what the real driving force of your will is, how that affects the choices you make in your life, the consequences of those choices, and how it influences the way in which you communicate with others. You will discover what elements of your throat chakra's power give credence to the profound messages contained in the quotes for this chapter.

Our being comes to this earth with specific qualities encoded in our souls. Philosophers such as Plato, spiritual teachers such as Caroline Myss and Eckhart Tolle and even the well known psychiatrist Carl Jung have made references to these soul imprints as archetypal energetic entities. For those of you who have biologically had multiple children, it is obvious how different each child is. For those of you who have not had this experience, think of the children in your extended family or of your friends and colleagues. Not only do all of these children look different, with the exception of identical twins, but all of them have different aspects to their personalities, temperaments, and wills; each child will perceive their life experiences, influenced by their archetypal patterns and their wills, in their own way. If you have siblings, think of the traits of your siblings and the significant differences there are between you and them.

Then there is the aspect of the beliefs that we have been taught that have been incorporated in the formation of our wills. Let us face it, we all have been steeped in tribal and societal beliefs, whether we are aware of it or it is something for us to discover. Those beliefs have an impact on the truths we hold ourselves to; they set the bar for us or draw a line in the sand, which we will or will not cross. We have already explored some of those beliefs and have realized the effect they have had on our lives. The combination of the qualities of our wills that we come into physical form with and the beliefs we have been taught are major components of our will. These combined factors result in the choices we make in life and are often based in instinctual survival impulses, egoic-centered beliefs, and the illusion that we are separate from our Creator.

There is a broad continuum of how we view what we may call our wills and the wills of others. Yet, as with all our judgments, they are based on our particular standards. We may label a person as a strong-willed person and choose to consider such as a positive quality according to our standard. Conversely, at the other end of the spectrum, we may label a person as a namby-pamby, which undoubtedly for some is a negative quality. Someone else might choose to use other labels to describe the same person, for example, as stubborn instead of strong-willed on the negative side and humble instead of namby-pamby on the positive side.

It is clear that we will bring our preconceived judgments and personal beliefs to the forefront when choosing the label we will assign not only to others but, what is more important, to ourselves. How would you describe your will? Take a few minutes here and make a quick list in your journal of words that you associate with the description of your will. Then make another list right next to it with words you think other people would use or have used to describe you. Be as authentic as you possibly can when choosing the words you believe others would use to describe your will. You might want to consider asking others how they would describe your will to get a more objective observation. Whether you base your comparisons of the two lists on how you think others describe your will or how others did describe it, note whether the descriptions you used to describe yourself are the same as the others. If not, there could be some really brilliant gems hidden there for you to explore.

The inconsistencies in the lists may be the starting point for determining what aspects of your will result in your life choices not being authentic with who you know yourself to be. When you make choices that are not congruent with the Truth of who you are, you lose your personal power and sabotage your integrity and your congruency with your soul. It is essential — let me repeat — it is essential that you uncover what other powers have control over your will and the choices you make. When you make incongruent choices, it is essential that you uncover what you based those choices on. Here are a few things to think about that might trigger what is really causing you to compromise your integrity and the congruency of your soul: a lack of courage to "step into your power" because of the changes it would create in your life and the responsibility you would need to take on; a fear of being humiliated if you attempt to go against conventional wisdom; a lack of trust in Spirit to support an endeavor you have dreamed of doing; or a fear of being alone when taking risks.

I Am Not the Doer

As I have already shared with you, one of the most profound methods of getting beyond fear is to use your life experience to remind yourself that you have been and are continuously surrounded by Divine grace and the presence of Spirit, even when you have been wholly unaware of its presence. You have undoubtedly heard the expression, "Let go and let God" and may have questioned whether this belief is a realistic approach to life. Five little words, none of them bigger than three letters, are so simple that a child just learning to read could easily get through them. Their childlike simplicity reminds me of another of Christ's teachings, "Become like little children." When I think of children, I think of their openness to life and all that life has to offer them in the present moment. Their innocence allows them to embrace each day with joy and a sense of enthusiasm, adventure, and wonderment.

The Yaqui shaman I spoke of before told me that you could break down the word *innocence* into "in no sense," in other words, get out of your head and the illusion of your mind. Another popular saying, "Keep it simple, stupid," has a similar message to share with us. These catch phrases can be life changing when we embrace the deeper meaning of what they represent from a spiritual perspective and are willing to live by their wisdom. How do we get beyond our minds and engage the power of our wills to trust that we will be caught if we jump into the proverbial abyss of the unknown by letting go? Much easier said than done when we believe we are the "doers" rather than the instruments on which life is played.

When we place ourselves in the role of the doer, we burden ourselves with the false belief that we have the power of total control over our lives. Furthermore, when we lose control of our lives, according to our standard, there is a tremendous sense of disappointment in ourselves and our ability to accomplish what we set out to do. When we know we are the instruments on which Creator plays, not only do we have the assistance of the resources of the universe, but we are also conscious that we are not alone in our undertakings.

When I deeply reflected on some of the most challenging times in my life, those times when I felt I would never be able to handle the enormous fear I was experiencing or regain my sense of self, I remembered that things did work out for the greatest good in my life, even though I could not have imagined a good outcome at the time. In retrospect, those episodes felt like an initiation by fire to a new state of awareness to the Truth of who I was. At the time, however, I felt I was out on a limb over a cliff and could hear that limb cracking. Now, when I become aware that I am slipping into fear and need to take control of a situation from that place of fear, I step back and remind myself of the wisdom I have been blessed with from those experiences. I am never alone, never! I am reminded of when I was able to surrender my will and need to control a situation to a power greater than myself.

I use my own experience as the yardstick to measure my ability to align with the power of Spirit and take a measure of my spiritual growth by trusting in Spirit. After all, can we truly measure our growth in any other way than through our growth from our experiences? I have shared this method with family, friends, patients, and clients for years. It has always resonated with them when they reflect on their life experiences with an openness to receive the wisdom those experiences granted them.

Your experiences are the only real means of determining that you have undoubtedly been surrounded by Divine grace even when you were not aware of its presence at the time. Reading about Divine grace and God's presence, attending workshops, and listening to other people's stories about miraculous experiences in their lives — even from people we know and trust — will inspire us. They encourage us to "let go" of our fear and need of rigid control. Yet as the saying goes, there is nothing like the real thing. If you have already developed the ability to trust in Spirit and have been able to surrender your will to Divine will when faced with the unavoidable challenges of life, you might want to skip the next few paragraphs. However, if you have not yet become aware of the Divine grace that was present during those most trying times in your life as being the power to guide you through your current or future challenges, the following may prove to be helpful.

GOING WITHIN: Think of an event in your life that was exceedingly difficult to control, an event that you believed would have serious negative consequences if you failed to correct it. Spend some time now to be present to the emotions and beliefs you had then. Did you think you had truly lost your way and that many things in your life were crumbling around you? Did you have a sense of confusion and self-doubt about the choices and actions you had taken that had brought you to this crisis and paralyzed you with fear? Did the event result from your making choices from a place of anger, fear, or shame? Had that event caused you to be immobilized or disempowered and unable to move forward, or did it cause you to continue to lash out, only making the situation worse? Did you cling to the illusion of safety that, had you just tried harder and hung on, somehow you could make things work out? Did it feel as though the world as you knew it and your values and rock-solid beliefs were disintegrating under your feet?

Stop reading now, close your eyes, open your mind, and, more important, your heart to that experience. Connect with your emotional state at that time. Take this opportunity to open to this life event and all that it entailed. During your reflection, set your intention to be open to any and all Divine guidance and humbly ask for Divine grace to reveal the wisdom contained in the event. Take all the time you need. When you are done, write about your experience in your journal. While writing about what was revealed to you, try to stay in the flow of Divine grace so that you can move smoothly into the next reflection.

Now that you have reflected on the situation and the strong emotions you felt, reflect on the actions you took at the time. Did you reach out to someone for support, sharing your raw emotions with him or her? Many years ago, while trying to make one of the most important decisions of my life, to get a divorce, I reached out to someone I felt well connected to, my parish priest. I was looking outside myself for approval and validation of what I knew I had to do. The priest represented the authority of God and the church because of my beliefs at the time. I explained my situation in great detail and asked for his help in making the "right choice." I was utterly unconscious of my attachment to exterior authority and giving my power to that authority. His response was, "What do you want me to do, feel sorry for you?" As harsh as that response may appear, I much later came to the understanding that that response was exactly what I needed at the time. Rather than relying on any external power, it drove me much deeper within myself and connected me directly with my soul, as well as to Divine grace and guidance.

I also realized I did not need someone else's approval for what I knew was right for me. I stepped into my own empowerment.

Maybe you have had a similar response from someone you reached out to during a crisis in your life, someone you trusted deeply enough to share your vulnerability with and had a similar experience. Maybe that person's response was not as harsh as my priest's response, but their response left you with a feeling of emptiness and possibly even despair. Maybe the best that person could offer was, "Oh, you'll get over this. Why don't you take up a new hobby to get your mind off it?" You probably wanted to vaporize this Polly Anna into nonexistence. Yet their disappointing response might have been exactly what you needed for your soul's growth.

Look back on that difficult time when you needed to make a life-changing choice. If someone were to describe your life today to you at that most vulnerable time, do you think you could have heard what they had to say, let alone believed that it could be true? I am not talking about everything in your life being perfect now, all your physical or emotional wounds healed, and your life exactly where you want it to be. I am asking you to view your life realistically from where you are today. Would you have been able then to envision it as it is now? Reflect now on what beliefs, thoughts, or emotions you had at that time that kept you from knowing, really knowing, that there was an alternative power you could have accessed to guide you in making your decision. Write down those beliefs, thoughts, or emotions.

Now write about how this situation unfolded. Include whether it matched your belief at that time, turning out the way you thought it would. If not, to what do you attribute the unanticipated results? Did the outcome come under the heading of impossibility or something you could not have imagined at the time (what I refer to as "You couldn't make this stuff up if you wanted to.")? There certainly is some truth in the saying "When one door closes another opens." Did that happen to you? If so, what force or power do you attribute the outcome to now?

≈

My hope is that these deep reflections on the experience you chose to explore will lead you to discover that something greater than your understanding at the time was present without your being conscious of its presence. My hope is that personal wisdom was revealed to you and that you became aware that other forces were active during that challenging time. I hope you were able to embrace the wisdom of knowing, from your *own* life experience, that you can trust a power beyond your understanding that is a constant presence in your life. My desire is now that you are conscious of your willingness to open yourself and intentionally create a sacred space within your being to receive new awareness, that you will do so whenever you find yourself uncertain and need Divine guidance. The wisdom you gained from the experience you lived through will serve as a life tool for your future because you now know that there was a presence with you in those moments of your darkest fears and despair.

Imagine how your life would have changed in an instant had you known, truly known, that you would be fine and that you were being Divinely guided and loved unconditionally. Imagine how you could have reacted differently because of that awareness. Spend some time now thinking about how that event would have gone in a much different direction had you been aware of Divine presence and known you were not alone. Play out in your mind different scenarios that could have unfolded had you chosen to align with something greater than yourself. Think of how your life could have been if you had not had to clean up what followed in the wake of chaos because of your fear-based words and actions. You may choose to explore other traumatic experiences in an effort to gain more wisdom to support you as you move forward on your soul's journey. Open yourself to the Divine grace that surrounds you instead of the fear and reactionary, uncontrolled emotion that occurs when you attempt to control a situation from a place of fear.

The wisdom you gleaned from your reflection is a gift that you will be able to apply to varying extents to all the challenges that arise in your life. It will give you the courage to make choices grounded in this new awareness. As you move forward in your soul's journey, you can make choices knowing that every moment of every day of your life you are surrounded by Divine grace. You will be open to seeing that challenges may be disguised opportunities to grow in your awareness of always being supported, that help is always available to you when you reverently ask for Divine guidance, and that surrendering your will to Divine will is always an option. Your willingness and ability to stay centered in this belief will determine the outcomes of future challenges.

Remember the experience of going within, to that place of peace that is beyond understanding, before you move forward to take verbal or physical action in response to current or future challenges. Stop to pay homage to the wisdom you have received. Remember, you cannot un-ring a bell once you have rung it. Your response and the choices you make when you face your next challenge will set off a chain of events that responds to the quality of the power you engage for action. This is the universal law of action and reaction. You and you alone get to decide what power you will align with in your choices of thoughts, words, or deeds. I know from my personal experience that I am not always able to align my will to this unconditionally loving force in the universe as quickly and graciously as I would hope. One thing I know for sure, each time I am challenged, I respond in a wiser and more unconditionally loving way after redirecting my energy from fear to an awareness of Presence that is always with me. It is then that I ask for the power of Divine grace to illuminate the truth of the situation I face.

CHOOSING UNCONDITIONAL LOVE

I recently had an experience during a morning meditation practice that expanded my awareness of the connection between illuminated vision and the choices we make. The evening before the meditation I unexpectedly found myself with a person with whom I felt a bond but with whom I had also had a confrontational experience a few months previously. We had each perceived an event from a different perspective, and this led to harsh words between us. This confrontation created an emotional chasm in our relationship. We had been in each other's company since then, but things were cool between us, to say the least.

In retrospect, the unplanned encounter was truly a blessing. It set the stage for a healing for both of us. Whether it was the passage of time since our confrontation or the discomfort we individually felt within our being when we would unexpectedly see each other, we were able to reconnect that night. At the time, I was unaware of the deep energy shift that had occurred within me. I had made a choice to ask Spirit to help me release the feelings of nonalignment I was experiencing when we would see each other, and that choice may have opened a space that allowed for this healing.

As I was settling in to my morning meditation, I reflected on the amazing experience I had had with this person the night before and the healing that took place for both of us. I was filled with a sense of wonder of the synchronicity of the encounter and all the things that needed to line up for it to unfold. Carl Jung, the renowned Swiss psychiatrist, defines the true essence of the word *synchronicity* as any apparent coincidence that inspires a sense of wonder and personal meaning or particular significance in the observer. It is a perceived connection between two or more objects or events without any recognizable cause.

Tears began to flow gently from my eyes as I experienced the great unconditional love that had arranged for us to meet. That power surrounds each of us at all times. The tears moved down my cheeks, over my chin, and stopped at my throat. I could feel my heart open to a place of deep peace and a sense of well-being. I became aware that as my illusion cleared from my mind, a radical change had taken place.

To clarify the symbolism of this event, I will explain it in terms of the chakras involved. The third eye chakra is associated with inner vision and our minds. My closed eyes represented my interior vision, the third eye chakra. The cleansing water of my tears represented the cleansing, or illumination, of my inner vision and mind. The tears that flowed to my throat chakra also cleansed my will and allowed me to be centered in my heart, releasing compassion and unconditional love. That centering allowed a healing for us both. In meditation, I became aware that through the prayer and deep contemplation following my confrontation with the person a few months before, my inner vision had been cleansed. I had surrendered my will to

Divine will, thus allowing access to compassion and uncondi-tional love, which shifted my viewpoint of the event.

A thoroughly different perception of that confrontation was revealed to me, allowing me to choose love over egoic fear. I was able to view the event as a powerful opportunity to experi-ence how quickly I can still shift into fear and defensiveness in a moment of perceived threat. Spirit aligned me with this con-frontation to provide the opportunity of going within myself to request sincerely the revealing of the Truth of a challenging time. It cleared the illusion that my Monkey Mind had trapped me in.

The illumination of the illusion allowed me to choose com-passion and unconditional love — the emotions that showed up at that synchronistic meeting the night before my medita-tion — over fear. The experience I had in meditation drove my understanding deeper within my being. To make the event even more profound, shortly after the healing encounter, suddenly and unexpectedly, the person was no longer in my life. I under-stood that because we had both resolved our fears and com-pleted our lessons, our interaction was no longer necessary to either of us in our souls' journey.

We move from an egoic-mindset response to a particular situation to an unconditionally loved-based response when we choose to respond from a higher consciousness, the key word being *choose*.

THE FARMER

This is a good time for a story that illustrates acceptance and surrender to God as an observational response to an event instead of becoming trapped in a response dominated by fear, a particular expectation, and a need to control. This story made me fully realize that nothing is at it appears and that there is always a greater purpose to life than we realize.

There was a farmer who lived many years ago in a remote village in China. He had a prize stallion that he loved dearly. One day the stallion got loose and ran away. The farmer's neighbor heard about the farmer's great loss and came to comfort him. He said to the farmer, "I'm so sorry for your loss. I know how much that stallion meant to you. Your heart must be broken, and you must be concerned about how you will replace this animal that you need for your farm and your income." The farmer replied, "We'll see." A few days passed, and the stallion returned, bringing with him many other horses.

The farmer and his son built a bigger corral for all the horses. The farmer's neighbor heard the good news and ran to the farmer's home to share in the excitement of his good fortune. He said to the farmer, "I am so happy that this good fortune has come upon you and your family. You are an honorable man, and this good fortune is well deserved." The farmer replied, "We'll see." A few more days passed, and as the farmer's son attempted to break one of the wild stallions so it could be put to use on the farm, he fell off the stallion and broke his leg.

The farmer's neighbor heard of this event and again went to the farmer to console him. He said to the farmer, "I heard about your son breaking his leg. How unfortunate for you and your son. He will not be able to help you in your chores, and he must be suffering a great deal of pain. This will make your life more difficult." The farmer replied, "We'll see."

The next day the Chinese army arrived in the farmer's village and began collecting young men to go to war. They went to the farmer's home when they heard he had a young son, but because the son had a broken leg, they passed him by.

~

What would your life be like if you could maintain a connection with what "is" in the moment and the awareness that all is in Divine order when we are connected to the presence within? How would your life unfold if your choices reflected the wisdom you learned from your life experiences and from your responses to life's challenges? How would you choose differently because of the gift of Divine grace and its revelation that the events in your life unfold in ways you cannot anticipate?

My life has changed dramatically. I now know that when I consciously choose to call on Spirit's unconditional love to help me release fear, the direction my life at the time shifts and unbelievable things occur. When I am able to "let go and let God," accepting the present moment, the struggle to stay centered eases, and the outcome is never what I could have accomplished on my own.

I still struggle with my ego, passions, and a desire to control situations that, according to my plans, appear headed in the wrong direction. As long as we are in the physical dimension, or have a sense of separation from the One, we will always experience duality on some level — unless we are enlightened beings. When we are conscious enough to seek Divine grace actively, we can send forth a heartfelt request to unveil our limited view of the illusion we are interpreting and ask that we become aware, from a higher awareness, of what we are really experiencing. With the power of Divine grace, we will be able to surrender our narrow-sighted will to Divine will. We will then be able to open ourselves to the presence of Spirit, perceive the situation from a more illuminated perspective, and make our choices based on that higher perception.

Surrendering My Will to Divine Will

When you feel frenzied and worried about a perceived challenge at hand, questioning whether your life is going in the direction that resonates with what you know your inner being to be, or when you are consumed with any of life's endless challenges, stop to ask yourself this question: Is this situation mine to manage, or is it something that is beyond my control? Usually, when a situation involves an awareness that someone or something else needs to change and that you alone will make that happen, it is fairly certain that the situation is beyond your control because you are centered in your ego.

My experience has been that when I approach a situation with that attitude, I end up being identified as the "problem." If after serious prayerful reflection you believe the situation is yours to manage, make the choice to ask for Divine grace to guide you along the way, move forward with pure intentions, be as open to Divine guidance as possible, and monitor your progress regularly with contemplation. Remind yourself often of other situations where you were able to achieve a positive outcome for all involved because you remained aligned with what you knew to be true: that you chose to ask a power greater than you to be in control. Also remember the times you were able to stop resisting the surrender of your will and were able to move beyond a dualistic judgment of a situation. In other words, you consciously chose to align with Divine grace and had the courage to "let go and let God."

Think of something you have done in your life that you now fully regret. Really connect with the emotion of that situation. Remember how awful you felt when you became conscious of the results of your choices. Imagine someone asking you to do something similar at this point in your life. Now fully conscious of the harm your choices and actions can cause, do you think yourself still capable of repeating that action? More than likely you could not, because you are conscious of the result. In a non-emotional event, like putting your hand on a hot stove when you were unaware it was still hot, resulting in serious burns, do you think you could do that to yourself again, consciously knowing the results? It is really almost impossible to slip back into ignorance on this matter and not know what you already know. Once you know the sun is the sun, for example, how could you not know it is the sun? This is another scenario where you cannot un-ring the bell. I have often described wisdom as knowing what not to do because you did it and it did not work out.

Your choices moving forward on your soul's journey will undoubtedly be influenced by your new awareness of being surrounded by Divine grace, even if you have only a slight awareness. You cannot ignore the experience of realizing that something beyond you has played a role in the unfolding of your life based on the wisdom revealed to you during reflection on your life experiences. You will need to decide what your priorities will be when making choices. When you inevitably come to forks in the road that present you with opportunities to refer to other beliefs than those you unconsciously reverted to in the past, which ones will you base your choices on? Before responding to a situation, contemplate deeply which aspect of your consciousness you will choose to be the launching point for your decisions, whether those decisions affect your life on a large or small scale. All choices, big or small from our perspective, have consequences that will reverberate throughout the universe.

My experience with surrendering my will is that a space opens to receive a new element of Divine awareness that allows me to view the situation from a position that is not centered in my ego. When I am able to go deep within my being to the place of the Truth of who I am, attuned to the wisdom of the Divine, I am able to receive that gift of Divine wisdom that gives me new insight into the situation.

When we step back and think about our lives, what things do we really think we are in control of anyway? I find the only thing I have control over is myself, and even that is not a consistent occurrence in my life. The aspect of attempting to control the world around us by our will and according to the beliefs and standards we have determined are right is ludicrous. In the process of reflecting on some of your own life events in your previous reflections, you have become aware that what you thought should or would unfold in your life is not always the way things turn out. The wisdom you received from your own experience of Divine intervention in your life should help you in surrendering your will to the Divine because you are aware, firsthand, of the blessings that flow from the Divine that are beyond your comprehension.

This is not to be misunderstood to mean you should not engage in life or attempt to do the best that you can, but that you should be aware that your first thought and action should be to go within and humbly ask for Divine grace to illuminate the choices you need to make. You should ask how you can be the best instrument to bring peace and harmony into the situation you are encountering and not let your will become a barrier to receiving Divine guidance.

In your reflections and contemplations, were you able to discover that no matter how difficult episodes of soul growth appeared to be at the time, those episodes contributed to the awareness of your connection to Spirit? What aspects of the wisdom you were given will you choose to apply consciously to your life? By becoming aware that what you have blessedly experienced includes golden wisdom, you can now move forward in a much more present way. You have retrieved fragments of yourself and are more whole. Consequently, you are more congruent, able to be more present in your life and therefore more empowered.

I encourage you not to lose touch with these gifts. The choices you make as you move forward, more confident that you are never alone, will expand your ability to be more willing to trust the ineffable Presence that is the creator of your soul's journey on your return to union with that Oneness.

Now that you have a glimpse of the benefits of aligning with a power greater than yourself by reflecting on your experiences, some of you may ask, exactly who or what are we aligning with? We have touched on this in chapter two, but some of that information may be appropriate to review here.

As many other people have told us through the ages, it is possible to describe what God is not, but impossible to describe what God is. The force some call God is an experiential force, not an intellectual one. Can you put into words what love is, or even fear, for that matter? We would need to revert to similes or metaphors in a vain attempt to reduce these profound subjects to simple words, and that would not even come close to describing them. The inspiration to use the metaphor of water for Divine grace in the beginning of this book is an attempt to describe the cleansing flow of Divine grace through our chakras. The examples in chapter two of how others have attempted to describe the Oneness of the universe, such as Indra's net and the light of a projector for instance, are an effort to use human concepts to explain the Divine. Such concepts as God, Divine grace, unconditional love, and quietude within our soul are forces we need to experience to get a sense of what they are. This power is what you connected with in your moments of reflection. You cannot describe what it is, but you know you have been touched by it, sometimes in subtle ways and other times through profound experiences.

Another aspect of the choices we make is the way in which we chose to communicate with others. We must choose to speak from a place of honesty, integrity, and congruency of thought, word, and deed if we want to remain aligned with the Truth of who we are. Speak with humility and from a place of alignment with Spirit. Not doing so causes us inner conflict, consciously or unconsciously, and we lose our alignment with the Truth of who we are. We lose our inner peace when we do not speak what we know to be true.

When we communicate with others from a place of conscious dissonance, the consequences of what we choose to speak will be disharmonious, and the subsequent chain of events that follows will negatively resonate throughout whatever is associated with that communication. It has been said that we should think twice before we speak. The wisdom of that statement is something we should take seriously and embrace. We should take that second thought and go beyond thinking whenever we are unsure of the Truth of what we are about to say. We should go within and ask for Divine grace and guidance before we move forward with our communication.

An enormous body of work is available to us today to guide us along our soul's journey. We are able to access the extensive work of mystics from centuries ago as simply as entering the subject into an Internet search. There are numerous contemporary authors and teachers, more than I can list here, who offer the wisdom of the ages in a style that is in tune with the language of our time, presented in a way that is in alignment with the times we live in, without compromising the Truth. Truth is timeless. The writings that resonate with your soul will let you know which writings are aligned with Truth. Take advantage of the wealth of mystical teachings, past and current. We no longer need to be a monk or nun to have access to the Truth that will guide us to make choices that are in alignment with our soul as we travel on the path of illumination. Ultimately though, the greatest wisdom you will gain is the wisdom you are blessed with as Divine grace reveals the gift of Truth in your own experience.

What Power Will You Choose

From the Native American tradition is a story based on a Cherokee legend that illustrates that we are faced throughout our lives with the need to make choices. The story is about a young Indian boy, his best friend, and his wise grandfather. The boy was given a sacred drum as a gift. The boy was much taken by the drum. When the boy showed it to his best friend, the best friend asked to play the drum. The boy did not want to share his drum with his best friend, and yet he felt bad about not wanting to share his precious gift. The boy reacted out of anger due to the conflict he felt within himself and ran away from his best friend. He ran to his safe place, the place where he went when he felt frightened or confused; he was always able to be at peace there. Yet this time he was not able to be at peace with the situation and felt bad because he knew he had hurt his best friend. He thought of his wise grandfather and knew his grandfather would be able to help him with the problem.

So he went to him and explained the situation. He waited patiently for his grandfather's response. His grandfather was quiet for quite some time and finally shared with the boy that he too had feelings that made him feel as though two wolves were fighting within his being. One wolf was full of himself, filled with pride, arrogance, and selfishness, and the other was kind, at peace with himself, and generous to all. The grandfather went on to explain that the two wolves were always confronting each other, and that the boy had those wolves within him as well.

The boy was quiet for a long time, thinking deeply about what his grandfather had shared. The boy looked up at his wise grandfather and asked, "Which one will win, Grandfather?" His grandfather looked down with great love and compassion for his troubled grandson and said, "Whichever one you choose to feed."

The Yaqui shaman I spoke of before told me a similar story using two dogs instead of wolves with essentially the same message. Whatever animals are used to portray our inner struggles is not important. The question is, which of the two conflicting energies within will you feed? Will you choose values and beliefs that will be in alignment with your new consciousness, or revert to choosing the illusions your mind and ego create out of fear? If you choose the energy of your higher consciousness, that will be the energy you feed in the future. Remember that when you are confronted by fear in making a choice, relapse is bound to happen in changing any behavior, but know that it can be a part of recovery. So, be on the lookout for the negative energies of your mind and ego, for these energies may have crept back within.

If you do relapse to your past ways of dealing with conflict, take advantage of this perceived failure to learn from experience. Let me remind you that wisdom can be defined as knowing what not to do. This is because you did it, and you know firsthand that it did not work. I have heard Bernie Siegel, M.D., the author of *Love, Medicine, and Miracles,* say many times that "F" does not need to stand for Failure; "F" can be viewed as Feedback. When you do revert to your old patterns of choice, hold yourself accountable for those choices and take responsibility for them. Try to identify what caused you to relapse into your previous patterns or what kept you from making your choice from a place of openness and unconditional love. Maya Angelou, acclaimed American author and poet, tells us that when we know better, we do better. When possible, share your insights with the person or people affected by your less-than-stellar choice so that all involved may benefit from the experience, and possibly a healing will take place for all.

Another piece of information that may be helpful to you as you try to change your behavioral patterns is the work of Andrew Newberg, M.D., the founder of the Center for Spirituality and the Mind at the University of Pennsylvania, and Mark Robert Waldman, an associate fellow, therapist, and researcher at the same center. They describe how different segments of the human brain respond to different situations. The limbic system of the brain, which has been labeled as the reptilian portion of the brain, is associated with our emotional reactions, such as the "fight or flight" reaction. The frontal lobes, the more evolved portion of the brain, are associated with logic and reasoning. Each has neurological responses to events and challenges.

Newberg and Waldman have shared their findings from countless brain-scan studies and analyses in their book, *How God Changes Your Brain.* They write that no matter how accepting you are of others' differences or how unconditionally loving you may think you are, "There will always remain the remnants of a neurological exclusiveness and fundamentalism in your brain.... The struggle between good and bad, between tolerance and intolerance, between love and hate, is the personal responsibility of every individual on this planet. The question remains: Which wolf will you feed, and which wolf will you tame?"

GOING WITHIN: At the top of a new page in your journal, write the following words spread out across the page: "Core Beliefs and Values," and then the word "Keep," followed by the word "Release." Make a list of at least five of your core beliefs and values under the heading "Core Beliefs and Values." Close your eyes and go deeply within, with the intention of feeling the emotion connected to each of the beliefs and values on your list, prayerfully asking for Divine grace and guidance in choosing whether each one continues to serve your soul.

Apply the new knowledge and wisdom you were given during your reflection of each core belief and value, and assign a "keep" or "release" status to each. When you are done, create a ritual or ceremony that has meaning for you involving the beliefs and values that you become aware no longer serve your soul and that you have chosen to release. Be sure to be centered, inviting Spirit to be present as you create your ritual. One suggestion is to write each one you chose to release on separate pieces of paper. Thank each one for having served you, and then burn each one and release the ashes, being sure you appreciate how each one once served you and is now no longer needed. Offer a prayer of thanks for the values and beliefs you will carry forward on your soul's journey.

~

Remember that your will needs to surrender to the belief that your mind must go beyond egoic-centered thinking before you can have access to unconditional love, especially when you face a challenge and are in fear. Your mind and your will always make excuses for why you cannot do something you know you need to do and why you should not surrender. The mind does not like the sound of one hand clapping; the silence becomes too overwhelming. Make all your choices from the consciousness of first aligning with Spirit, surrendering your will to Divine will. Note that *you* have to take control of your mind and your will, or someone or something else will.

At the beginning of this chapter I shared with you Myss's statement that we choose to love conditionally or unconditionally. There I also posed a question: Is it love or our choices that contain the most power in our lives? After having read this chapter about your will and the power of choice, what is your answer to that question? Along those lines, I suggest that you reflect on which wolf you will choose to feed as you move forward on your soul's journey.

As we move to the next chapter to explore the heart chakra, bring the values and beliefs with you that you were Divinely guided to keep during your reflection. We will take them into the sacred chambers of your heart as we focus on Divine grace flowing into the recesses and crevasses of your heart.

CHAPTER 5

FLOODING YOUR HEART WITH COMPASSION BY THE RIVER OF DIVINE GRACE:

THE HEART CHAKRA

The pressure now is too strong. It breaks through and begins to flow into our broken hearts. Its cleansing waters of Divine grace fill the chambers of our hearts, wherein reside hurt, abandonment, mistrust, restriction, resentments and inability to forgive ourselves and others. As the chambers fill with the living waters of unconditional love, we begin to expand our awareness, our ability to forgive and the beginning of unconditional love starts to trickle in.

It is better in prayer to have a heart without words
than words without a heart.
— *Mahatma Gandhi*

Darkness cannot drive out darkness: only light can do that.
Hate cannot drive out hate: only love can do that.
— *Martin Luther King, Jr.*

THE QUOTE BY MARTIN LUTHER KING, JR., indicates that he was indeed connected to the enormous power of unconditional love and compassion. He was a great proponent of unconditional love and compassion, so much so that he lost his life because he championed mystical Truths, just as Mahatma

Gandhi did. He based his civil rights movement on the principles of Mahatma Gandhi's nonviolent movement of *Ahimsa* in India, which ultimately won India's freedom from the royal crown of England. *Ahimsa* was the foundation of Mahatma Gandhi's success. *Ahimsa* is a Sanskrit word from the Hindu Vedic scriptures. The essence of its meaning is to do no harm to any form of life, because all life contains God. King thoroughly believed in Mahatma Gandhi's teachings and the message of his life. I am sure that in times of discouragement during the civil rights movement in the South, he reminded himself of one of Gandhi's most powerful quotes, "When I despair, I remember that all through history the ways of truth and love have always won. There have been tyrants, and murderers, and for a time they can seem invincible, but in the end they always fall. Think of it — always."

King's belief in a nonviolent, measured response to the injustices that were being forced on the people he served inspired others all over the United States to march against the injustices that were being inflicted on the black community in the South. Some of you may have lived through those dark days of the civil rights marches and even participated in them. What enormous courage and strength of their convictions those marchers demonstrated!

Their belief was that unconditional love, Truth, and nonviolence are powerful forces. That belief saw them through those difficult days. Their unwavering faith did not falter; it carried them to their goal. They demonstrated that when we put our trust in the unshakable power of the compassion and unconditional love that resides within each of our souls, no matter how buried that love may be, it will always win out over darkness. When the people on the other side of that force come face to face with that power, ultimately they must bow to its presence. At the end of the day, that power moves mountains for the greater good of all. An open heart, centered in compassion and unconditional love, is power that is undefeatable.

COMPASSION AND UNCONDITIONAL LOVE

I have heard Caroline Myss tell the story of Christ's journey, some of the people he met while on the earth, and events that took place during the journey. She tells the story about Christ's journey with powerful, heart-centered words and deep emotion. I will try to convey the power of her words in sharing the story.

The night before Christ died, during his last hours, he was abandoned by his closest friends in the Garden of Gethsemane. He had been falsely accused, betrayed by some of those friends who denied even knowing him, and humiliated in a very public forum. The next day he was executed in a manner reserved for criminals. Christ endured every excuse we use to strike back at people. And yet, after all this brutality, while dying on the cross, Christ asked his Father to forgive the people who had crucified him, "for they know not what they do." The words he spoke on the cross were ones of ultimate compassion, unconditional love, and forgiveness. Christ also taught that we should love those who are our enemies.

GOING WITHIN: Let us take time to delve into the experience of being treated badly by those around us. Close your eyes and think of a situation where you felt you had been harmed. Maybe you have been abandoned by those you thought loved you, falsely accused of something you did not do, betrayed by a close friend, or intentionally humiliated by someone in public. Bring to mind incidences in your life that are similar to those situations. Connect to the feelings, thoughts, and your consequent actions. Shift your thoughts to where your emotions are now at this moment in regard to these experiences. Are the people who were involved in the events still in your life today? If not, why not? Remind yourself of the reasons you used to respond in the way that you did. Have you been able to forgive those involved, or were their actions against you beyond what should be forgiven? Write in your journal about the experiences you focused on, how you feel now about them, and how you feel about each of the people involved. We will reflect on these at a later place in this chapter so hold them in your thoughts until then.

Another mystic who epitomizes how the awareness of the Oneness of creation opens the heart to compassion for all life's beings is Mansur al-Hallaj. He was a first-century Iranian Sufi mystic who experienced Oneness with God and taught about his experience. Like Christ, who taught "I and the Father are one," al-Hallaj taught the same. Here is one of his writings:

I am the Truth — completely at one with creation
I saw my Lord with the eye of the heart
I said: Who art thou?
He answered: Thou

Similar to Christ, al-Hallaj's teachings were considered blasphemy during his life, and so he was tortured and crucified. He too uttered a prayer before he released his physical body; "Oh Lord, if you had revealed to them what you revealed to me, they would not be doing this to me. If you had not revealed to me what you revealed to me, this would not be happening to me. O Lord, praise to thee in thy works."

The current Dalai Lama is the fourteenth manifestation of

the embodiment of the Bodhisattva of Compassion. Bodhisattva is an enlightened being who is centered in compassion for all beings. An interviewer once asked the current Dalai Lama an emotionally charged question: how he felt about the Chinese who had killed so many of his compatriots and fellow Buddhist monks. His immediate, unequivocal response was: "Compassion." I believe that the Dalai Lama's response was based on his wisdom and awareness that had the Chinese who committed the acts of violence been aligned with the Truth of who they truly are, they would not have been able to commit those acts. The Dalai Lama "sees" the suffering of the Chinese and realizes that it must be so severe as to render them capable of inflicting atrocities on their fellow human beings. Thus, his answer of compassion says it all.

It is the same Truth that brought forth Christ's response at His crucifixion, "Forgive them for they know not what they do," and al-Hallaj's prayer at his crucifixion. These enlightened beings, Christ, al-Hallaj, and the Dalai Lama, are all rooted in the same sacred wisdom: when someone is living in the conscious awareness of the Truth of who they are, it is impossible to be anything but unconditionally loving. Therefore it is not possible to interact with life in any other way. Christ taught that we should love our enemies and changed the old law of "an eye for an eye" to unconditional love. Mahatma Gandhi said, "An eye for an eye makes the whole world blind." Again, the illusion that we are separate from God, each other, and all life forms, creates a fear that motivates us to act in ways that are not in alignment with that which we truly are. When our reality is based on our separateness from God, we live our lives in a fear-based paradigm.

Notice how Christ and al-Hallaj were heart-centered, as is

the Dalai Lama — personifications of compassion, unconditional love, forgiveness, and reverence for all life. Christ's words of loving His enemies, al-Hallaj's words of seeing God through the eye of his heart, and the Dalai Lama's embodiment of compassion are teachings of the importance of an open heart. They are words of wisdom that direct us to the fundamental path of illumination of our souls. Christ and al-Hallaj were, just as the Dalai Lama is, sacred evolved souls, each capable of holding the highest consciousness of Oneness, no matter what was or is going on around them or to them. Each was or is able to feel compassion for the suffering of others who cannot reach and live in that highest consciousness and stay centered in unconditional love. I know of no alternative way to reach alignment with the Truth of who we are, other than through the heart. An open heart allows us access to compassion, unconditional love, forgiveness, and reverence for all of life, and we become conscious of our Oneness with God and the interconnectedness of all life.

Human beings have a flawed consciousness when they are not in alignment with the sacred Oneness of creation. That flawed consciousness renders them so frightened and separate from the consciousness of Oneness that they may descend to a state of darkness. That darkness renders them capable of doing the most inhumane things to other life forms they view as separate from themselves. They are capable of those atrocities in a futile attempt to feel powerful and in control of their surroundings. In reality, they are far removed from their power when they act from that level of consciousness. They attempt to hold steadfast to their world in the only way they know, with their egos being the center of their universe. They attempt to protect themselves by controlling everything around them, fully unconscious of that impossibility. These few examples show the beliefs they hold to justify outlandishly cruel behavior based on fear. The beliefs have resulted in the torture, crucifixion, and slaughtering of thousands of people throughout the history of humanity and sadly, continue today. This is the extraordinarily destructive power of fear.

GOING WITHIN: After reading about some of the events in the life of Christ, al-Hallaj's writings of seeing God through the eye of his heart, and the Dalai Lama's compassion about the killing of his compatriots, go back to your journal writings about the events you selected regarding being mistreated by others.

Review those writings, and reflect on the events you focused on. Although the transgressions you experienced are unlikely to approach the inhumanity of the above examples, they were nonetheless traumatic for you. Close your eyes, go deeply within, and humbly ask for Divine grace to reveal new insights into the situations you wrote about. Have any of your feelings or awareness of those situations changed? If so, write about what changes took place in your awareness. Did the compassionate way of the responses of Christ, al-Hallaj, and the Dalai Lama to their offenders help you to view your traumatic events differently? Did knowing that it is impossible to act out negatively when someone is aligned with the Truth of who they are influence your thoughts? Were you able to connect with the suffering of the souls of those involved in your trauma? Could you relate to the disconnection they must have been experiencing that allowed them to take the actions they took against you? Do you think you would want to handle your responses differently now when similar situations arise? If so, write about why.

Have you experienced an opening in your heart that was not there before you reflected on the responses of the three enlightened souls? If so, write about that opening and how you will nurture its growth. Be sure to write down the new insights you were blessed with and apply them to your life as you move forward on the path of illumination. Those insights may be crystal clear to you right now, but they can quickly fade when you reenter your life and are challenged.

~

The insights are sacred gifts, gems of wisdom given in response to the situations you reflected on, but they are also gifts of wisdom you can use on your continuing journey to smooth out the rough terrain on your path. Holding our center in the space of compassion and unconditional love when we are being assailed is no easy thing to do, but knowing the suffering of the soul of the aggressor when centered in fear and not in alignment with their Truth can help us respond with compassion.

Putting Compassion into Action

Now that you have deeply reflected on Christ's, al-Hallaj's, and the Dalai Lama's compassionate response to their offenders, remember the event you called to mind in the last chapter that you now fully regret. Remember your own experience of acting out when you were not aligned with the Truth of who you are and the resulting consequences of your unaligned words or actions. Your experience will help you to understand that the *suffering* of offenders result in unaligned behavior, because in your situation you were the offender. You have the potential to awaken to the deep Truth and sacred wisdom of compassion.

As the consciousness of compassion grows within you, *compassion* is no longer simply a word to be used lightly, now that you are becoming more and more aware of the profound sacredness of its meaning. Spend as much time as you need as you move on with your life, reflecting on your own experiences to grasp fully the cause and effect of acting or speaking in non-alignment. As your awareness increases of the unconscious suffering of your or other beings' acting out of nonalignment, your foundation of a consciousness of compassion will lead you to an ability to love unconditionally and to the blessing of an ability to forgive yourself and others. The words of Christ while on the cross, "Forgive them for they know not what they do," now speak to your soul from a sacred space. "Compassion," the Dalai Lama's response to oppression and al-Hallaj's words at his crucifixion, "Oh Lord, if you had revealed to them what you revealed to me, they would not be doing this to me," will come from that same sacred space within your very soul.

As I stated previously, the heart chakra is the center of unconditional love and compassion. Joseph Campbell describes the heart chakra as the place of our spiritual birth, the center of transformation. *Om* is the Sanskrit syllable within this chakra. It is held to be the most sacred of all syllables as the sound of the energy by which all things are brought into manifested form. Campbell teaches that *Om* is the sound that is *not* made by two things hitting together: all things make sound when they hit something; even air that passes through the resistance of our larynx makes the sound of our voice. *Om* is the sound of the transcendent. Some say that *Om* is the "word" that is referred to as the beginning of creation in the Christian bible; "In the beginning was the word, and the word was with God, and the word was God."

Compassion and unconditional love are the strongest powers we possess, and yet they are the most humbling as well. Hatred constricts life; compassion and unconditional love expand life. Hatred disrupts life; compassion and unconditional love harmonize life. Hatred darkens life; compassion and unconditional love illuminate life. Compassion and unconditional love coupled with forgiveness are powerful energies. As the saying goes: to err is human, to forgive is divine.

In Asian medicine, fire is the element that rules the heart. Yet fire can also influence our minds when we are consumed with emotion: passion, meaning anger, rage, or obsession generated in the heart. We can become obsessed with controlling the world around us, which renders us out of control. Campbell taught extensively that desire and fear are the two consistent obstacles we must subdue on our journey to becoming fully whole. Both of these obstacles take us into the realm of illusion and duality. Obsessive desire for power, wealth, sexual conquests, prestige, material possessions, or anything that takes our hearts away from unconditional love is to our detriment. We become driven by our lust for more and more and get farther and farther away from our inner life, leaving us angry, miserable, and unsatisfied because there will never be an end to the need to fuel the burning fire of our "heart's desire" from the negative place of self-centeredness. We become isolated because we are not able to connect with others in a loving way because we only see them through the eyes of what can they give me that I need to feed the insatiable fire within.

This internal inferno blinds our perceptions of the world around us and our misery is projected into the world, coloring everything we come in contact with. Our toxic emotions create a self-fulfilling prophecy that the world is a dangerous and scary place with not enough to go around. We are constantly watching out for signs that people are out to get us or use us, so we push others away; our distrust of our fellow humans confirmed by our perspective of their motives. We harbor our hurts and disappointments in the sacred chambers of our heart, as we do not have the capacity to view our surroundings from a different perspective. We become stuck in a self-imposed constricted life. We are not able to move out of our own way to engage in life in a positive way, and we are unable to give of ourselves; therefore, we do not have meaningful relationships that can nurture and support us.

Unconditional love aligns us with the Truth of who we are. Every time we chose fear, we are separated from that Truth and are in the realm of duality and illusion. Carl Jung tells us that our awareness will become clear when we look within our heart. That when we look outside ourselves, we can become enmeshed in "dreams." When our focus is within, we "awaken." The dream aspect of his words is in alignment with illusion and duality; the awakened aspect is in alignment with the Oneness.

Newberg and Waldman, the neuroscience researchers I mentioned in chapter four, did research on "ways to generate empathy between people, especially when their beliefs are oppositional." They explain that previous research had discovered that "right" eye contact builds what they call neural intimacy and trust. They have found that most people avoid making eye contact with people they do not know. They designed a study that paired complete strangers, had them face each other, close their eyes, and focus on someone or something they "deeply loved." They reported that in less than a minute, the participants began to smile. The researchers noted that the muscles that surround the eyes of the participants softened as they kept their eyes closed. Then the researchers instructed the participants to open their eyes. They found that 95 percent of the participants felt at ease when they opened their eyes and found a smiling, welcoming face before them. When the experiment was conducted without a period of contemplating a "deeply loved" object, 70 percent of those participants who had made eye contact with a partner felt ill at ease.

I am sure many of you have experienced both versions of this experiment. I know that when I am walking down a street, preoccupied with something and not in the present moment, I usually do not make eye contact with people. Those times when I am centered and present, I consciously try to smile at strangers I pass. More often than not, most people return my smile. Give it a try to see what results you have. You may be surprised at what you learn. Just a simple smile is enough to create a positive reaction in most people. Unfortunately for people who are closed off, they cannot respond to others even when the other is reaching out to them.

Many times, people like this are unconscious that they have created the hell they are living in. They are caught in a trap, like an animal running round and round on a treadmill but never getting anywhere because it is always running in the same circles, journeying on their well-worn path of unhappiness, deeper and deeper into their broken hearts. They cannot recognize the goodness in the world, because they are consumed with their view of the disappointing life they have created by their thoughts, aligned as they are with their belief of separation and fear. They cannot give unconditional love, the thing that they desperately need to do to connect them with the world around them, because they have none to give. People caught in this circle of fear are not aware that unconditional love does not limit you; it expands your world to living more of it and living it more fully. Conditional love limits and constricts your life and your soul, putting unnecessary constrictions on your life. Most times a crisis will show up in their world. What little control of their lives they perceived of having is gone. That loss can bring them to their knees. This loss can also be a wake-up call and a blessing in disguise. It can bring someone over to the loving side of life instead of the fear-based life they have been living.

Out of desperation they reach inside of themselves, asking for help from something they have lost contact with a long time ago. They surrender to the faint memory of internal peace and stop their outward search for fulfillment. They feel an ever so slight connection to that peace and are able to take a deep breath for the first time in a long time. Exhausted from the struggle of trying to keep everything in their life under control, a trickle of light is allowed to appear and can begin to seep into the sacred chambers of their hearts. This small trickle is sometimes enough to begin the release of the need to be in control of everything and arouse the search within for another way to be in their lives.

OPENING TO UNCONDITIONAL LOVE

Perhaps these people begin to feel the natural enthusiasm for life that was once a part of them, which opens them to connecting with others near them. Fresh relationships develop, bringing them closer to being present in life. They have a new view that opposes their old view that everyone is out to get them. And so the unfolding of this life moves forward from deep darkness of the soul to the God-given gift of the light of unconditional love. Knowing that love extinguishes the burning flame of desire and fear. The soul of this heart is now set ablaze with the fire of passion for wholeness and a return to the Truth of who they are, of being one with the unconditional love of God.

Whether we are aware of it or not, we are continually showered with universal unconditional love. We all yearn for it, yet many of us search for it in the exterior world. All spiritual masters have shared its Truth with us. They live in alignment with unconditional love, and their lives emanate that power. Unconditional love purifies the energy of our hearts, where our emotions are centered. When we experience universal unconditional love, even for the tiniest fraction of a second, our consciousness changes. It is no longer possible not to know that this power exists in our universe. Our heart is expanded and is touched by a power that is beyond description and our reasoning ability.

Even this brief encounter carves a deep desire in our hearts that drives us to reconnect with the force of unconditional love. Its essence is so alluring that we quickly become addicted to reaching for its presence. Its pure bliss and peace are truly beyond our comprehension, yet we recognize it, and it humbles us to our core. We feel blown over by a force that is not of this world. This is the nature of the power and essence of universal unconditional love. The reason this force is so alluring is because we recognize that something profound has touched us, something that is vaguely familiar. Our hearts open to the essence of the Truth of who we are, and we get a whiff of our oneness with the One.

This deep yearning that has been carved in our soul is the desire to return from whence we have come. This intuitive pull is the call of our journey to return to that unconditional love that unites us with our transcendent self. The theme of unconditional love and sense of wanting to return from whence we have come has been written about for ages. There have been songs composed to try to express it, and it has been symbolically painted by great artists, all done by people whose souls were on fire with the desire to share their experience with us and awakens us to the enormous power of unconditional love that is within all creation.

WHOLENESS AND A RETURN TO TRUTH

Every desire we have is basically a desire to feel better about some aspect of our lives or ourselves. My experience has been that even though many of my desires did not result in what I thought at the time would be advantageous to my life, the desire itself was a reaching out to become aligned with the Truth of who I am. The desire was based on the underlying yearning to become one with the Oneness, even though I was not conscious of it at the time. The desire may have appeared to be the farthest thing from a spiritual desire, but in retrospect, it was yet another illusion that facilitated the progress on my journey home. It is similar to the principle of the *neti, neti* journey I described in chapter two. May I again emphasize that there is no greater illusion than the illusion that we are separate from our Creator. That powerful illusion is the genesis of our desire and our longing for union with where we came from: Oneness.

Unconditional love is one of the driving powers of the universe and is our natural state of being when we are aligned with the Truth of who we are. We are made of God's unconditional love: it is the core of our souls at the time of our making. When we feel empathy with someone who has had a major loss or for someone who is facing a major challenge, our thoughts, feelings, and words effortlessly flow from the core of our beings, our hearts, in an effort to comfort and support that person. When you take the time to send someone a note of appreciation for something, have you noticed how effortlessly your words flow? Where do you think the inspiration for the words comes from, and why is it so easy to find the words that convey your deepest feelings of appreciation to the other person? The words and feelings pour forth from us because we are responding to the vibration of unconditional love that is the core of our soul, our true nature.

Let us look at this from the opposite end of the spectrum of emotion. How would you express appreciation for the assistance someone gave you, knowing that he or she had undermined a project you were working on together? What would your thank you note say if you were aware that the gift of time or material the person had given you was based on an obligation that the person felt they needed to fulfill? Certainly you can feel the stark differences in your thoughts, feelings, and words in this second scenario if you are not centered in unconditional love. How much effort would it take for you to express that appreciation and write that note? More than likely, the words would not flow easily, and you would need to reach for appropriate words, words that allow you to remain authentic, which is not an easy task. The resistance we feel in those situations results from not being attuned with our natures.

Now, think of a situation when you were upset with someone. Ask yourself whether you were upset because the person did not meet your expectations, which made you choose to withhold unconditional love. If you are choosing to do so, be conscious of a decision not to be in congruence with the Truth of who you are. Ask yourself, what is unconditional love asking me to do in this situation? When you hear the answer, what is your first response? If you resist following through with the answer that came to you, ask for Divine grace to release your resistance so you can return to your wholeness. Can you see how your giving unconditional love is for your benefit in all situations? Undoubtedly, this is not always easy to do, but when we look at the effect that not giving unconditional love has on us, we might want to rethink our position.

I know of no better or more efficient way to get into alignment with the Truth of who we are than through an open heart, which allows us access to the unconditional love and the compassion it contains. When we are not capable of connecting with that power, we come from a place of illusion and inconsistency. Our misguided beliefs result in our judging others. We tend to make judgments according to our individual rules and regulations about what is and is not acceptable, what is right and what is wrong on any given day. These rules and regulations shift as our life experience expands our knowledge base and therefore our perspective. There is absolutely no consistency in these judgments. They vary from day to day and from culture to culture. By virtue of the fact that these judgments are inconsistent, it is self-evident that they are not based on sacred Truth, because Truth does not waver.

WOMB OF OUR SPIRITUALITY

Caroline Myss refers to the heart chakra as "mission control". Joseph Campbell calls it the place where our "spiritual birth" takes place. Llewellyn Vaughan-Lee, a Sufi mystic and the author of *Love is a Fire,* calls the heart "the womb of our spirituality." All the wisdom and self-knowledge revealed by Divine grace thus far on your soul's journey have illuminated the light attributes of the chakras we have explored: the crown, third eye, and throat chakras. This wisdom and self-knowledge need to flow through the heart into our lower chakras to infuse them with those gifts.

The heart chakra navigates the power from our upper chakras through its energy field and imbues that power throughout the lower chakras. The lower chakras are primarily connected to our interactions with the exterior world and are influenced by our human impulses, instincts, and tribal beliefs. You can certainly see why Myss, Campbell, and Vaughan-Lee, profound scholars of divinity, would label the heart chakra with such powerful words: "mission control," "the place of our spiritual birth," and "the womb of our spirituality." Eckhart Tolle has said that the sun may be shining outside, but if the window shutters of your house are closed, you will remain in darkness. I take this to mean that if your heart is shuttered tight by your mind and your will, you will remain in darkness to the Truth of who you are, and all your interactions with your exterior world will be based in that darkness of unawareness of the Truth of who you are.

My journey has awakened me to a particular awareness. All the workshops I have attended, all my traveling to holy sites around the world, and all my study with some of the most conscious teachers on the planet today, though wondrous and enlightening on many levels, were not sufficient to truly transform my life. Only when I was willing to choose to open my heart to fearless, unconditional love did that happen. For me, the cracking open of the floodgates of my heart, which I had closed tightly in the illusion that I would be able to protect myself and keep my life safely in control, brought transformation.

It was not enough for me to "know" through my intellect the teachings of the masters. I needed to experience the Truth of their teachings in my heart, to go deeply within my soul to remove the obstacles to that Truth, and then put that awareness into my daily thoughts, words, and deeds. That is what transformed my life. I cannot tell you about one specific experience that opened my heart to the Truth, but I know that Divine grace has guided me through the process every step of the way. Sathya Sai Baba, Indian guru and philanthropist, taught that you never know which strike of the rock will break it open. I have always kept that teaching in mind when I or someone I am speaking with is discouraged about a lack of progress on the soul's journey.

My experience is that once your heart has been opened and connects with unconditional love, you will no longer be able to close your heart to that connection with the indwelling presence of Spirit for very long. The power floods your heart. You will never be the same. Nothing will be worth the price of choosing to separate from the bliss of the Divine that you experience when you are centered in unconditional love for you have unwittingly developed a relationship of devotion to this powerful force. In other words, once you experience the opening of your heart with unconditional love, it is impossible not to know of its existence and magnificent blessings. You will not be able to contain this power within yourself but will have a burning desire to share that love through empathy and compassion with others who are struggling with the challenges that life presents. You will develop an attitude of reverence for all of life. You may not be able to stay completely centered in amazing Divine unconditional love all the time, but you will make every effort to return to its bliss. Nothing will stand in your way of being present to its call.

Marianne Williamson, best-selling author and lecturer, in her book *Return to Love*, goes into great detail about the enormous blessings that occur when we chose to surrender to uncondi-tional love. She states that *Return to Love,* based on *A Course in Miracles* mentioned in chapter one, says that we have two basic emotions: fear and love, and that all other emotions derive from those two. When our hearts are centered and open to unconditional love, we automatically bring acceptance, com-fort, encouragement, hope, joy, nurturing, and support to all of life. These emotions are just a few of the qualities that emanate from us from our connection to unconditional love, support-ing the well-known adage "Love heals all wounds." When we close our hearts, fear brings such emotions as anger, the urge to control, envy, jealousy, mistrust, and suspicion. We are then unable to experience joy or even the unrestrained laughter of children. We can open our hearts to love or keep them closed out of fear. As always, the choice is ours.

Fear is the lack of awareness and connection to our Source. It signals a sense of separation from God, or the essence of who we are. Fear can be defined as the opposite of love or the illu-sion that we are separate from the One. Thus, we are back to the illusion of duality, where our ego resides. Tolle has written extensively about how limited our lives are when we choose to come from a place of ego or from the illusion of separa-tion from the Oneness of the universe. On the other end of the emotional scale from fear is love, Divine love being beyond what most of us think of as love. Many people throughout the ages have defined God as love and hold that God and love are one and the same. However you attempt to define Divine love and God, it will be futile because it is beyond human under-standing and reason.

SENSING DIVINE LOVE

This is the same as the other aspects of God that I have discussed in this book; it is an experiential event, not a conceptual experience of the mind or intellect. Divine love is a portal to a different dimension than the love that we are familiar with, the love of a family member or friend, or "falling" in love in a romantic sense; Divine love is something that happens "to" us through the power of Spirit. I have experienced moments of unconditional love. I know, beyond a shadow of a doubt, that it was the Source of my being bringing me home. I do not mean the end of my physical existence on planet Earth, but rather being called within to a place of Divine love that then radiates to my surroundings and all those around me.

Think of the expansion you feel when witnessing a magnificent sunrise or sunset. Your limited world expands when you take that beauty within and you connect with a feeling of inspiration. You are not aware of a constriction such as you may have felt previously; you are in the present moment and drawn into the beauty that has been laid before you. You had nothing to do with the majesty of the sky, and yet here you are: a recipient of its beauty. Have you not found that limiting thoughts and worries disappear during precious moments of viewing a spectacle of radiance? Such is a minute experience of Divine love. Divine love overpowers your limited mind and awakens you to the world beyond your fears and resistance because you have become connected to your Source.

In these moments of exquisite beauty we are not thinking of any of the things we feel we do not have enough of: recognition, appreciation, material possessions, power, or any of the trappings of illusion that we think we need to be satisfied with our lives. We are not caught up in the competition to have more;

for a few brief moments the competitive drive of "not enough" that runs our lives takes a back seat in our minds. Our open hearts are in the driver's seat, without any effort from us. We have a feeling of inclusion in rather than exclusion from our surroundings.

You cannot experience fear and love at the same time; they cannot coexist. You cannot walk backward and forward at the same time. You cannot feel the emotion of happiness and despair simultaneously. Similarly, you cannot experience feelings of expansion and constriction within your being at the same time; it is impossible. You cannot be aligned with who you truly are and have thoughts or perform actions that are out of alignment. It is just not possible. Think of a time when you were centered in an open, loving heart space. Remember where you were and who you were with. Bring those precious memories into the present moment and relive the wondrous expansive feeling of that time. Now, try to imagine that you were able to commit an act of violence. Do you think that could even be possible? It is the same impossibility of it being night and day at the same time in the physical realm of earth.

FORGIVENESS, THE COMPANION OF COMPASSION, AND UNCONDITIONAL LOVE

The handmaiden of compassion and unconditional love is forgiveness. First, we need to probe why we have perceived someone as harming us and in need of our forgiveness. Is there an element of being in the illusion of our perspective of this transgression? Try to get to the core of the situation to determine whether our perspective is accurate or whether we are the one who is in error because of our mistaken understanding of the situation.

Possibly this was a case of someone not meeting our expectations or standards of how we thought things should have unfolded in the world. Do we hold someone else to standards we ourselves cannot maintain consistently and then shut our hearts to them, knowing full well that we are not always capable of offering unconditional love? Mother Teresa of Calcutta describes the less-than-perfect ways we behave as "distressing disguises," a perfect way to identify how we appear when we are separated from the Truth of who we are and of how we can perceive others when the same applies to their state of awareness. If, after a self-assessment of our perspective, we indeed still feel the situation requires our forgiveness, we need to come to a place where we have an understanding of what forgiveness is, what it is not, and what it does.

I am sure most of you have heard the common analogy for not forgiving someone you believe has hurt you in some way. I write this for those of you who have not heard it, as I think it is a really good way to express the issue from a purely selfish perspective. *Not forgiving someone is like drinking poison and expecting the other person to die.* The hurt and sorrow we carry within our heart result in our paying the price for the burden of the disharmony and negative energy of the situation. You can see plainly from the analogy that forgiveness is really a gift we give to ourselves.

In the horrific killing of five young girls in the Amish community of Nickel Mines, Pennsylvania in 2006, one of the Amish farmers responded to a question about his community's ability to forgive this atrocity with heartfelt wisdom. His answer was, "Acid corrodes the container that holds it. That's what happens when we hold onto bitterness." His response is an example of his deep understanding that forgiveness is a gift we give ourselves.

The sense of constriction and withholding of our loving natures are clues that we are holding back unconditional love. We will be the ones to pay for that negative energy within our being, including our physical selves. Therefore, forgiving someone can really be a selfish action. When we forgive someone, we really are forgiving that person for our benefit, given the toll that not forgiving them will take on us. Conscious of the alternative outcome for ourselves, forgiving others is the much wiser choice.

When we forgive someone it does not mean we condone what he or she has done to us or that we accept the harm done to us. We need not even have an ongoing relationship with them. We forgive them from a place of unconditional love and focus on our awareness that they have been created from the same Source that we have. We come from a place where we are aligned with the knowledge of the Oneness of creation, from the place of the wisdom of the soul. We are aware that others may be incapable of being in alignment with the Truth of who they are.

If you still hesitate to offer forgiveness when you know it is needed in your life, ask yourself if you are willing to pay the price for holding on to your disconnection from the essence of who you are. When you choose to allow yourself to forgive someone, you release the emotional pain and suffering that you have kept within your heart. If you are in a situation where you can reach out to those involved in this disharmony, you have the added blessing of releasing them of the negativity they are experiencing in the situation.

GOING WITHIN: You know you can be blessed with the alchemical process of releasing whatever is holding you back from the consonance and peace within as you have experienced this before in the previous contemplative reflections in this book. As before, close your eyes and humbly ask for Divine grace, with a sincere heart, to reveal the wisdom contained in your resistance to let go of your hurt and forgive. Take your time and review the issue that is holding you back and then open your heart to the wisdom that will be gifted to you. Be sure to write about your experience in your journal for all the reasons previously stated. Hopefully, you have an expanded understanding of what forgiveness is and through your reflection you were able to feel the release of held onto constrictions in your heart through the power of forgiveness. Here is another of Mahatma Gandhi's quotes to inspire you when you know you need to forgive but may be fearful of taking that step, "The weak can never forgive. Forgiveness is the attribute of the strong."

~

SEEING THE WORLD THROUGH THE EYES OF GOD

In her memoir, *Eat Pray Love*, Elizabeth Gilbert wonderfully describes her journey of self-discovery and the importance of being heart centered. One of many heart-centered scenes in the movie based on the book that really caught my attention and that she describes so beautifully in the book was the experience she had with a ninth-generation Balinese medicine man, Ketut Liyer. She visited the medicine man previously when she was in Bali on an unrelated assignment for a women's magazine. When she returned on her second visit, Ketut showed her a sketch of a figure he had drawn during a meditation session he had had. The sketch is an androgynous figure with no head and four legs. The four legs were to stand on, but in a position like a human rather than an animal. The head was represented only by foliage for hair. The face was drawn in the chest area near the heart and both its hands were depicted in a prayer position, palms together over the heart. The sketch was given to her, and Ketut told her what the sketch meant. The figure has four legs to keep one firmly grounded in the earth dimension. He told her not to view the world through her head, as he ran his fingers over the wild foliage that takes the place of the figures head. He then pointed out the eyes of the figure that are drawn in the figure's chest over the heart. He told her that this is the way she should view the world, through her heart, so she can know God. What a beautiful way to express how we should view the world that surrounds us.

The enlightened souls I have used here as examples of being centered in unconditional love — Christ, al-Hallaj, and the Dalai Lama — certainly viewed the world from their hearts and from the point of view of seeing God all around them, as depicted in Ketut's sketch of the androgynous human figure. They are beacons of hope for us as we move along on the path of the illumination of our souls. However, I sometimes become discouraged when I cannot stay centered in my heart and keep it open all the time. I find it difficult to do consistently on a daily basis even though I have been on a serious spiritual path for decades. Strive as I do to stay heart centered, I still have periods when I become locked into my shadow. As Ralph Waldo Emerson, American essayist, lecturer, and poet, told us, "We have a great deal more kindness than is ever spoken," and that is the truth. Fortunately, I am able to acknowledge my shadow energy visits fairly quickly. Although I take responsibility for the consequences of the presence of my shadow when

I become aware of it, I am discouraged when I slide into the shadow side of my personality.

Rumi tells us that our task is not to seek love, but merely to seek and find all the barriers within ourselves that we have built against it. It is a gift of wisdom that helps us to remove the barriers that have formed scars in our broken hearts, allowing Divine grace to flow in, cleanse the sacred chambers and caverns of our hearts where sorrow and despair are buried.

There are a few things I can be thankful for that are gifts from my shadow, however. First and most important, it keeps me in check by keeping me humble when I slip. It shows me where my vulnerabilities are and where I need to focus my improvement efforts. It lets me know how I need to direct my prayers when asking for help from the Divine. It also provides me with opportunities to practice compassion and forgiveness for myself. This is the most challenging thing for me to do, as is true for many others. However, it is essential that we forgive ourselves for our errors. The more we are able to do so for ourselves, the more we will be capable of forgiving others and demonstrating compassion toward them. *After all, we cannot give something to others that we do not know how to give to ourselves.* I also believe that whenever possible, we should take responsibility for any harm we have done to others directly with that person or persons, except when we believe it might do more harm than good to the other.

CREATING A SPACE TO RECEIVE THE DIVINE

My husband and I have had the honor of having a Lakota Native American sweat lodge on our land. During one of our sweat ceremonies, the Lakota leader who leads the ceremony was doing his visioning for each of the people in the lodge before the close of the ceremony. When he came to me, he said I had a "missile" coming toward me and that it would be powerful. Often the specifics of the messages this man receives are symbolic and contain no specific details. Such was the case for me that night. The next morning I just felt like staying at home and reading instead of going to a Sunday morning service with my husband. I wanted to continue reading a book about St. John of the Cross. I had been introduced to St. John's writings on a group trip to Avila, Spain, a few years previously with Caroline Myss.

I want to give you some background information before I continue with what happened to me the morning after the sweat lodge ceremony. Myss had an overwhelming experience with St. Teresa of Avila while she was on stage lecturing on mysticism in Chicago. The experience was so powerful that she needed to leave the stage. I happened to be present at that lecture. It was not until our class returned for the second session of the course on mysticism a few months later that Myss shared with us what had happened to her. She explained that St. Teresa came to her on stage that day and that the experience changed her life. She told us that she was now writing a book about St. Teresa's classic writing, *Interior Castle*, and that the title of her new book would be *Entering the Castle*.

James Finley, a clinical psychologist and former Trappist monk whom I wrote about in chapter two, also lectured to our mysticism class. A few years later, Myss arranged for a small group trip to Avila, where she was to lecture on St. Teresa while Finley would lecture on St. John of the Cross, who was one of St. Teresa's spiritual directors. We also were able to tour places that St. Teresa had lived. I was somewhat familiar with St. John's work but felt very drawn to him after listening to

Finley speak so lovingly about his life. Saint John's most well-known writing is his poem "Dark Night of the Soul," which is mentioned in the introduction of this book. Needless to say, the trip was astonishing and laid the groundwork for what was to come.

Now I return to my reading about St. John of the Cross on the morning after the sweat lodge ceremony. This experience, like all explosive personal experiences, loses much in the telling because it is such a personal event, with more meaning for the individual than for others. I relate it in the hope that St. John's heart-centered teaching will flow into your heart with love.

The author of the book explained that some of the theologians and authors at the time of St. John questioned how "Christian" St. John really was because he did not specifically include Christ's name very often in his writings, which was a common practice during that time. I went on to read that St. John had taken a different path. He introduced his knowing that we need to create *nada*, which literally translates from Latin as "nothing" or "space," in our hearts and souls to receive the *todo*, which translates as "everything," or the gift of God in our hearts and souls.

This awareness hit my heart and soul like an explosion. Yet it was not until I stopped sobbing that I was able to realize what had happened. This was the missile I was told about the night before that would come at me. A missile had indeed pierced my heart and soul deeply. When I regained my composure, I knew that I needed to create more and more *nada* in my heart and soul before I could receive what I had been seeking my entire life: the *todo*, or the totality of the presence of God in my heart and soul. The way St. John had framed this message (or "missile") was in the exact words I needed to hear. These did indeed hit me like a missile and crack me open. I needed to purify my heart in order to receive this precious gift. I cannot begin to explain to you the effect this awareness had on me for days. As I write about the experience now, I can feel an aching in my heart because I can feel the Truth of St. John's words. He must have already experienced what I felt to be able to let us know how to receive this most cherished gift.

I want to share with you additional information about this beloved mystic. He came from humble beginnings, was devoted to God and Christ, and throughout his life deeply yearned for union with the Divine. His fellow Carmelite monks had captured and tortured him because he wanted to reform the lenient lifestyle of the Carmelite order at that time, just as St. Teresa was doing with the Carmelite order of nuns of which she was a member during the time of the Spanish Inquisition. He endured that torture for nine months before he was able to escape. He did not strike out at his fellow monks but instead went deep into his soul. It was during this time that many of his mystical writings occurred, including "Dark Night of the Soul."

Saint John was in love with the unconditionally loving God of his understanding and not with the punishing, fearful God that I had internalized as a child. Saint John encouraged us to open the door of our hearts and let this Lover into the depths of our soul.

To open our hearts suggests creating the space, *nada,* therein. This is the writing of St. John that struck such a chord deep within me. Making space in our souls and emptying *ourselves of ourselves* creates a path for Divine grace to flow into our souls in preparation to receive Spirit. Saint John refers to the presence of God as "companionship and inner strength, which walks with the soul and gives [the soul] strength." The more space we create to accommodate this companionship, such as removing our prejudices, judgments, or past hurts and humiliations, the more Spirit can dwell in our hearts and souls. The more space we make within, the more room there is within our beings for unconditional love, compassion, forgiveness, and reverence for all of life.

Our minds and our wills tend to become trapped in the illusions of our exterior lives, and we then are not free to receive the very thing that will set our hearts and souls free, unconditional love from our Creator. We are easily trapped in our self-centered desires and fears, leaving our minds to take over our lives. We need to be mindful and on constant alert. Our desires and fears creep up on us, and before we are aware of this invasion, it has control over our behavior. As mentioned previously, St. Teresa referred to these desires and fears as reptiles that come into our souls in the darkness of our shadow energy. We are unconscious of their arrival until it is too late.

We become mindful of their presence when we become aware that we have lost our sense of peace and joy within our beings. The justification of our fears and self-preoccupation allows our minds to take us down the path of illusion, wandering in the land of endless circles of self-pity and isolation that feed on themselves. Cut off from others and our souls, we become unable to feel God's unconditional love for us. As we struggle with trying to find our way back to alignment, we realize we have lost our way. This is not necessarily a bad thing, but we are unaware that the feeling of being lost is necessary for our souls to grow. In St. John's words, "To come to what you know not, you must go by a way you know not." Trust and surrender are key for this journey. So you can see that going back to where you were, comforting as you might think it would be, means that your soul will not travel farther on the path of illumination.

THE DISTANCE FROM THE HEAD TO THE HEART

The journey of the soul is the journey to the Source of the Truth of who we are, that long distance from our heads to our hearts that we have previously explored in chapter four. Along the way of this arduous journey, when we have created space in our hearts, we discover the liberation of our souls by God's tremendous river of unconditional love and compassion flowing into them. All mystics from all traditions speak of this journey from their own deep experience of the transformation of their lives as they transcend their self-centered consciousness to universal consciousness. This is the essential journey, Self calling to itself, Spirit calling to our spirits. We may decline to surrender to the journey and attempt to run from our hearts' inner call, but remember: *No one has ever escaped his or her shadow by running from it.*

We must be patient with ourselves and wait for Spirit to fill the space, the *nada*, that we have created in our hearts and souls with the ecstasy of Divine love and union with our Source. When Spirit finds *nada*, Spirit enters. We need to let go and get out of the way, having faith that we will be filled with Divine love and grace. Know that the Divine heals your history and brings you whole into the present, where you can fully participate in the joy of God's freely given gift of life.

As we move into the next chakra, bring your conscious awareness of unconditional love of others with you, but most important, the unconditional love of self, since the place of the self is what we will be exploring in the next chapter. Now, think of the heart chakra we have just explored as the birthing of illumination to the next three lower chakras. Keeping in mind that all the chakras interact and affect one another, these next three chakras are more connected to how we interact with our outer world than the upper four chakras we have already explored.

You have an opportunity to give birth to the wisdom you have received in your previous reflections to the lower chakras, knowing that this wisdom will change your life. To give birth is to bring something that is within (for example, new consciousness) to the external world. The three lower chakras, for example, as Myss and Campbell teach, are more related to our exterior world. So we will now "birth" the wisdom from our illuminated upper inner chakras to our more animalistic, lower — external — chakras. Or, you can stay where you are in your soul's journey. The choice, as always, is yours.

Chapter 6

Cleansing Your Sense of Self with the Purity of Divine Grace:

The Solar Plexus Chakra

The Divine grace that guides the flow of this water is now trickling into our solar plexus chakra, which holds our self-esteem and intuition. We are opening and trusting that the cleansing waters of Divine grace are washing away long-held beliefs of separation from our Creator. Our consciousness is becoming open to the knowing that we can navigate the flow of our life from a higher and gentler way of being in our earthly experience. Guidance is trickling through, and the cleansing waters of Divine grace are clearing our resistance.

To be still is to be conscious without thought. You are never more essentially, more deeply, yourself than when you are still.
— *Eckhart Tolle*

This above all: to thine own self be true.
— *William Shakespeare*

THE SOLAR PLEXUS CHAKRA is connected to our sense of self, otherwise known as our self-esteem. Our self-esteem begins at a very early age, that time when we begin to be cognizant of what other people think of us. We get input from those around us about what favorable qualities to have and what undesirable qualities are. The people around us do not necessarily need to articulate what they think of us. Nonverbal expressions can give us input just as easily. When we identify our self-worth with input from outside our self, we give our power away, and our sense of self is based on someone else's opinion of us, over which we have no control.

The solar plexus energy center is also associated with our intuitive self, discerning the world around us from an ethereal field rather than from the manifested realm. There are times when we sense or feel what is happening rather than having a tangible base for what we perceive. Many teachers refer to this as our "gut reaction" because we really have nothing concrete as a basis for that reaction of something that just does not feel right. It can be defined as a knowing without rational thought. We often have an immediate sense of being comfortable with someone we have just met or a place we are in that is new to us. These intuitive "knowings" are different from the Divine guidance we receive. These intuitive messages are on more of a physical level, while Divine guidance comes from a higher level of consciousness.

FOLLOWING YOUR GUIDANCE

As you give more attention to the intuitive messages you receive, you will be more sensitive to your instincts. You will also be capable of trusting your intuition. Your sense of self is now fairly grounded in the knowing of what you consciously choose to be the foundation of your beliefs and values because you have explored the wisdom of the previous four chakras. You will know whether the intuition you are sensing resonates with what you now know to be of the utmost value to your being thus far on your journey.

In the solar plexus chakra we will explore values and beliefs centered in integrity and your ability to hold yourself to the standards you choose as the guiding principles of your decision-making process as you interact with the exterior world. After you establish those principles, you will intuitively sense when you are not in alignment with them, compromising yourself, thus losing your center. You will intuitively feel when you are losing your center, when you are not in congruence with your beliefs and value system, and when this is taking place, you will be able to acknowledge it consciously. You will be able to take corrective steps because you now know that you can go deeply within yourself to ask for Divine grace and guidance to illuminate how to regain your center. The alternative is feeling lost because you are losing your footing and do not know what is happening to you.

Each time you have the courage to follow the guidance, intuitive or Divine, or both, and to act on it without attachment to the outcome, you will know that a greater purpose is being served. You will receive confirmation that you are guided by a power greater than yourself. That confirmation, or affirmation, can come from within as a sense of knowing your choice was appropriate because you sense the energy of alignment. Exteriorly, what is needed to fulfill your choice will line up in unexpected ways. The more you attune to the process, the more you become unshakably sure that you are never alone in any situation or endeavor.

It is essential, however, that you stay in the consciousness of integrity and in congruency with what you know to be the Truth, that you make your choices wisely, and that you "follow through." I have found that when I center myself in the awareness that "I am not the doer" and surrender to the thought that "I am here, Lord, if you need me," I am capable of extraordinary things. Again, the key is keeping yourself centered in the awareness that you are the instrument and not the doer, that with God all things are possible. On the other hand, you cut off your ability to receive Divine grace flowing to you when your egoic mind takes control of the action because there is no space for you to feel Spirit enter. Your ego fills that space, and your focus is on the need to be right or to be acknowledged for something you have done: that is the outcome you are looking for. That focus deprives you of the gift that the Divine could have given you, a gift far beyond what your limited vision for the outcome could possibly have imagined.

SELF-ESTEEM FROM WITHIN

As I have said earlier here, this energy center is also where we carry our sense of self, more commonly known as self-esteem. In the beginning of our lives, we primarily get our sense of self from others, what our family thinks we are, based on their judgments and beliefs. When we are not in alignment with those beliefs, they will emphatically tell us what we should be or do to be aligned with them. As we move out into the larger world, there is no limit to the input we receive about who we are in the eyes of others. Our self-esteem is therefore a cumulative process over the course of our lives, changing as we grow chronologically, intellectually, socially, and, most important, spiritually.

Self-esteem is necessary for us to function in the world and for us to have full and productive lives. A lack of self-esteem makes us vulnerable to inevitable shifts in the external world, and it is easy for us to get caught up in fear-based thinking and actions. We then begin to perceive the world that surrounds us as an unsafe place, that perception becomes the basis of our interactions with our surroundings, including all our relationships. This way of engaging with the world sabotages our endeavors to improve our surroundings and to hold on to the dreams we have for ourselves and our destiny. We begin to doubt our abilities and ourselves. We lose self-confidence and are drawn into the world of feeling we are not "good enough."

Quickly, considering that your first thought is usually your best thought, and without judgment, choose five words to describe your personality and help to define who you are at this time. Write these words in your journal. We will review them later.

After reading about what a lack of self-esteem can do to our lives, we can understand that it is essential for us to have a clear awareness of what principles we use to establish the foundation for our self-esteem. It is vital that we be conscious of the values and beliefs we identify with personally and choose to integrate them into our personality. More important are the values we will abide by in our soul. It is also essential to determine whether those values and beliefs are based on the vacillating beliefs and ever-changing values of the world outside our self or on the values and beliefs that we identify with that are based on the Truth of who we are in our interior world.

There is not a distinct cutoff between our two worlds — our exterior and interior worlds. These worlds interact with each other continually and can often create conflict within. It is important that you are able to align both your interior and exterior value and belief systems to avoid losing your center and sense of self. For example, if you are faced with the choice of telling the truth about an incident, knowing that if you do you could lose a friend, your job, or some other part of your life that you value, that decision would need to be aligned with the Truth of who you are; otherwise you will compromise yourself and pay a *soul price* for your decision.

GOING WITHIN: We need to go deeply within these systems and identify which of our current values and beliefs support our false sense of who we are based on the world outside ourselves and which ones support our *soul selves*. When we examine our values and beliefs, releasing those that no longer serve our souls, a higher authority rises to the forefront, and we initiate the disengagement process from our false sense of self to the Truth of who we are. As we free ourselves from false qualities and liberate our true selves, we will become aware of the attributes of serenity, joy, centeredness, and humility that are rooted firmly within our souls and are guiding our lives. When our self-esteem is based on our awareness of our connection to the Divine, we are self-assured and empowered from within, no longer needing approval or validation from without. Our integrity and self-worth will be intact, and we will be at peace with ourselves and the world around us.

How do you identify yourself when someone asks, "Who are you?" Where do you go to connect with your sense of self? Take time now to write down in your journal at least five core beliefs on which you base your sense of self. This process is worth the time you invest in it as it will reveal to you the effect these beliefs have had on how you have navigated through your life. Now write about how the beliefs came to be the foundation of who you know yourself to be. Give an example of how at least one of the beliefs played out in your life. The amount of effort you put into this reflection will be rewarded when you discover what the driving forces of your life have been. When the time comes, we will explore the beliefs and the five words you previously recorded that describe your personality.

≈

Releasing the Beliefs
That No Longer Serve Your Soul

As I noted before, we are socialized very early in life to identify the objects in our surroundings: this is a cup, this is a pan, this is money, this is beauty, and so forth. As we get a little older, we begin to comprehend the value those objects should have in our lives, according to the people responsible for our well-being. We are taught, or learn by observing our role models, that some things are good and some are bad. The values placed on the objects depends on how caught up in duality and illusion our role models are. Our family or caretakers do not necessarily articulate these values, but the message nonetheless comes through their actions and reactions to their environment, and we observe them. My experience and observation show that we become more and more products of our environment as we insidiously internalize the values we have witnessed.

When we experience these things for ourselves, independent of what our family and authority figures try to tell us about what is really important in life, we start to pick and choose what we will keep as our beliefs and what we will reject based on their value to the life we want to lead. Little do we realize that we have swapped most of our family's and authority figures' values for the values of the new tribe we are identifying with, our schoolmates, and friends.

This process goes on and on as we incorporate the values we think are important to us into our belief system, based on our own perspective of the reactions from those we interact with. In this system, the measuring tool we use to determine our self-esteem at this point in our lives tends to be based on our external world instead of our internal world. Most of us fill our cup of self-esteem with judgments of what is valuable: material possessions, personas, relationships, and so on. The value of those judgments is based on these standards. We measure our success by the amount of money we have, our level of education, our jobs or careers, the status we have in our society, how beautiful we are according to the standards that are in vogue at the time — too skinny, too fat, married, single, divorced, children, no children, our wardrobe — and on and on and on as we mature. "Our cup runneth over" with our beliefs in "stuff" and appearances.

There is no room at our inn for our souls, the elusive thing we really are searching for, peace beyond human understanding and the resulting sense of wholeness. We have not created the space that St. John wrote about, so Spirit cannot fill that space in our soul. When we base our self-esteem on the belief in the Truth of who we are and when we have been graced with the experience of that Truth, our attachment to the things we own or value becomes a burden we are no longer willing to carry, nor are we willing to pay the price it demands from our souls. When we become more than willing to release the beliefs that are oppressing us with their weight, we then have the ability to create the *nada,* or space, to be blessed with *todo,* God's all-powerful unconditional love. Our lives will never be the same.

I have found that when I am able to base my sense of self on my connection to Source with the help of Divine grace, I have the courage to do anything that has been placed before me. I am then centered on the knowing that I am not the doer, that something greater than myself is directing this play I call my life. I always have to be aware of not sliding into my egoic consciousness, however, as that can certainly put an end to my ability to receive the flow of Divine guidance. I have already given examples of this happening to me in the course of my life in ways I was never aware of until I was so off-center I could not help but to take notice that I had lost my connection to what holds my center.

~

As you become more aligned with the Truth of who you are, you will become more sensitized to and aware of any imbalance of your energy centers, or chakras. You will be more trusting of your intuition or "gut reaction," more trusting of this communication because your self-esteem is now firmly grounded in your internal beliefs. You are no longer floundering. This is similar to what St. Teresa referred to as "building a scaffolding for your soul" to support you. Nothing will rock you from your foundation, because your foundation is grounded in Truth.

Each time you have the courage to follow Divine guidance and act on that guidance without attachment to the outcome, you will become more steadfast in knowing that a power greater than your ego is motivating and directing you. The more you attune yourself to that power, the more you will realize, really knowing, that you are never alone. You will have confidence in your endeavors when you stay in the consciousness of "I am not the doer," surrendering to Spirit. Strive to *empty yourself of yourself*, so that you may become the flute on which the Master can play a wondrous melody. Again, create the space of "I am here, Lord, if you need me."

When you attach your sense of self to "I did that" or when the need to be right is of the utmost importance to you, then you automatically know that the egoic mind is in control. When the egoic mind is in control, fear is automatically in the forefront, and the slippery slope of illusion can consume you. Your heart becomes constricted, and the resistance to the flow of the stream of Divine grace begins. As soon as you become aware that you are losing your connection with the Divine, stop, and go within. Take whatever time you need to reconnect and retrieve your solid foundation. You now know from your own experience when your ego is in control. Your growing awareness of everything working out for the greater good in Divine order when you have surrendered your will to Divine will allows for you to call on Divinity more easily. This belief will become the new compass by which you navigate through life.

OUR BELIEFS DRIVE OUR ACTIONS
A TRAUMATIC EVENT

To demonstrate how profound the effect of these beliefs can be on our lives, let me give you an example of one core belief of my identity that I held about myself for more than five decades of my life.

I have previously shared with you that I was raised by a single, alcoholic mother, boarded out as an infant, returned to live with my mother, and then orphaned at sixteen. I share what now seems a somewhat melodramatic life experience in the hope of helping you to find the gold in the lead, in alchemical terms, in your own life experience.

My mother's predominant words of wisdom to me were, "You're tough, you're just like me, and you can take it." That was the mantra that always went through my mind during difficult times in my life. The really odd thing about it was that I never asked what "it" was that I was tough enough to take. I just filled in the blank as I went along. As I reflected on that mantra many decades later, I realized it was my mother's way of trying to protect me from the pain she identified with in her life. That one sentence reverberated through my being and was the cornerstone of how I approached life. I was very proud of being tough. I wore that belief, internally and externally, like a badge of honor. Unfortunately, that mantra shut me off from the things I should have addressed. My life certainly would have taken a different course had I had a better sense of self.

The following is an example of how our beliefs drive our actions. When I was in my first year of high school, I was fairly heavy. This contributed to my already significant lack of self-esteem. One day during the lunch period, a girl I did not particularly care for was sitting at a table with the people I usually had lunch with. I put my tray on the table, pulled out my chair, and began to sit down as this girl intentionally pulled the chair out farther from the table without my realizing it. I proceeded to sit down. As you can imagine, I ended up on the floor and heard nothing but laughter around me. This was an urban public high school. News traveled fast throughout the cafeteria and continued through my school day, throughout the school.

I waited for this girl after school, which was near Main Street in my city. When she came around the corner onto Main Street and out of sight of the school, I grabbed her, threw her to the ground, and began to bang her head against the curb of the sidewalk. I was filled with rage at having been humiliated in such a public way. Fortunately, a friend who was with me pulled me away from the other girl. I can only imagine what might have happened to both of us had my actions continued. I might have caused a head injury, or worse, she could have died.

My friend and I went home to my house. I was pretty shaken up but had a sense of "She'll think twice before she messes with me again!" My mother was at home at the time, which was unusual. She took one look at me, knees cut up and scraped open from being on the sidewalk, and asked, "What happened to you?" I admitted that I had been in a fight, expecting my mother to yell at me. I was sure I was in deep trouble.

My mother said, "I've got one question for you." I waited for what felt like an eternity, for an explosion to hit me. I was so scared I did not even have a single thought about what that one question could possibly be. Then she asked the one question. "Did you win?" I just stood there in silence. I was taken back because I expected a storm of anger from her. I was speechless for a few seconds, and then I heard myself say in a soft voice, "Yes." That was the end of that conversation. The situation was never discussed again. That interaction between my mother and me fit her belief that I was indeed tough like her and could "take it." At the time, I never imagined how disastrous her pride and silent approval of my destructive behavior would be in my life for my life's future journey.

This example demonstrates how I automatically reverted to "tough" action, which was a deep belief I carried in response to someone humiliating me. This was my way of protecting my image and myself. It was important to me that the girl in school and others would know better than "to mess with me again." As I write this, I can hardly believe I am writing about myself. Can this be me?

You can see from my example how detrimental beliefs can be when they are not aligned with the Truth of who we are and how unconsciously we use them to protect ourselves. Given my situational action example of my extremely destructive belief, on which I based a huge portion of my self-identity, you can surely understand the effect it had on my life and on the lives of those around me. I know my mother loved me dearly. That may be hard for some of you to believe. Nevertheless, I know that her reaction was her way of showing me how to protect myself. It was how she had learned to survive her traumatic life. For many decades, believing that I needed to be tough served me. Indeed, it helped me to survive other tragic events in my life. Unfortunately, the impact that operative belief had on those around me was destructive, and I left a wake of chaos behind me. To make matters worse, I was unconscious of the chaos I had inflicted on them.

A SECOND TRAUMA

In my mid-fifties I unconsciously created yet another drama in my life that really rocked my world because I had spent an enormous amount of time and energy on *going within* and attempting to connect with my soul. The event was nowhere as destructive as the drama of the high school event had been, but it was nonetheless one of not being in alignment with who I thought I was. Of course, I was unaware that this was a crisis of my own doing. I could not believe that at this late stage in my life I was feeling such a magnitude of devastation in a way that felt far too familiar to me. After I had picked myself up off the floor, having lain there in a fetal position sobbing, I vowed that I would reconnect with my soul and that this time I would be consistently committed to a spiritual path and a community for support and direction. Here is the story:

To make a long story short, I attended a workshop given by Margaret and David Hiller, "Supporting People To Express Their Magnificence." In addition to attending the workshop, I signed up for a one-on-one session with Margaret Hiller. This was a big change for me. Usually I would have signed up with a male instructor. I am not clear about why I was drawn to males in situations like this one, but I have a sense that my choices were driven by an unconscious need for a father figure. This new choice was an example of my staying committed to making changes in my life. For a home project for my one-on-one session with Margaret, I was instructed to make a collage or write phrases on a large poster about things that reflected only my positive aspects. This reflection was very challenging for me.

When I tried to write about my cherished badge of honor, being tough like my mother, I froze. What I can describe only as a moment of Divine grace illuminated my consciousness and revealed the negative hold my belief had on my soul. I realized in that instant that the belief had to go. I was also left with such a void within my very being that it felt like a cavernous hole within my psyche. My heart had opened up, and I was being swallowed by the void left. Who was I if not this tough person? How could I function without this persona? I was truly disoriented and at a total loss as to how *to be* in this world.

As though this sense of an identity crisis were not enough, the next wave of my undoing came over me. I was filled with an awareness of how disloyal I would be to my mother — whom I believed to be the only person in my childhood who had truly loved me — if I were to drop this mantra. This cleansing was almost too heavy for me to bear. How could I consciously choose to be so disloyal to her memory? The feeling of disloyalty to my mother, whom I loved dearly, was suffocating. I knew I had to release this belief that no longer served my soul. I prayed for the courage to keep the space open in my heart and asked for it to be filled with a new belief. Yet I had no idea what that belief would be. It had to be Divine grace that would give me the courage and insight to recognize this pivotal moment in my life. The decision was all mine to make. I knew I had no option. I had a sense of what might happen to me if I did not release the old belief. It was more like a stark awareness than a factual knowing.

Opting to write phrases rather than make a collage, I picked up the marker and tearfully wrote, "I don't want to be tough anymore, Mom, and I don't want to 'take it' anymore." I could barely breathe from the fear I felt wash over me. Then, without even an instant passing, a sense of quiet and unbelievable peace enfolded me, and I knew beyond a doubt that I had made the right choice. I know this event sounds melodramatic, but I must tell you that choice changed the direction of my life in ways I could never have believed. Over time and with many synchronistic events, I shifted that old belief and replaced it with faith in a power that protects me from within, the awareness that I am never alone and that God's Divine love and grace are always available to me.

Exploration of your core beliefs can be revealing and in many cases can result in profound changes in the course of your life. As with most things in life, there is a hidden treasure to be found in our experiences if we are willing to become vulnerable and open ourselves to going deeply within. I hope this sharing has shed light on the essential need to reflect deeply on the five basic beliefs you wrote about.

Going Within: Let us first reflect on the five words you chose to describe yourself, and then move on to your five beliefs. Review the words you chose without deep thought or filters of what you thought were the right words to write. Humbly ask for Divine grace to guide you through this process. Reflect on them now and get a sense of how you feel about these words. Do they give you any insight about where you get your sense of self or self-worth? Are you satisfied with them or would you like to change some of them because you have had an opportunity to reflect on them? Feel free to do either but be sure to write, for each one, why you choose to keep them or change them. Write about what thoughts or associations surface for you that shed light on how you perceive yourself to be. Be sure to do the same for any new words you choose.

Now explore the five core beliefs you wrote about. Please give yourself the gift of spending time contemplating the effect they have had on your life. Take one at a time, examining it with any new insights you have received since you wrote it. Ask yourself whether your thought process immediately went to the beliefs you hold about your exterior identification, such as your job, ethnicity, marital status, or gender, or whether you went to the realm of your internal world for the beliefs that are the foundation of your sense of self. This is an important distinction and will give you an awareness of which beliefs have the most power over who you believe yourself to be, those of your inner world or your exterior world. Identify what makes you feel disempowered. Then identify what makes you feel empowered.

It is essential that you do not contaminate this process by introducing blame *(be-lame)*. Be careful not to blame anyone or anything for your choice to include a particular belief in your value system or for your behavior in the past. Doing so would undermine the very self-esteem you are trying to bring into your being. Remember that whenever you blame a person, an incident, or a religious organization, for example, for something you have done, you give your power to that entity, which weakens your sense of self, your self-esteem. This results in taking on the role of the victim.

I encourage you to delve beyond your mind's concept of who you think you are and to explore the realm of your true identity. Again, humbly ask for Divine grace to reveal the hidden gems of wisdom, the positive and negative aspects of what you want to change, as you reflect on where these beliefs came from and what made you include them in your sense of self. Do you want to make some adjustment, major or minor? Given the content of the concepts you have just read about, do you feel your beliefs need some refining, or do they need to be eliminated completely and replaced with something new that serves your soul from a higher level of consciousness? There is no wrong or right here. It truly is about how each major belief serves your individual soul's growth on its journey of illumination.

After you spend time in contemplation, ask yourself whether you consciously want to keep these beliefs, edit them, or release them to make space for new beliefs to identify with. Trust the Divine guidance you receive as well as your intuition from the energy center we are exploring, and drill down into what resonates with your soul. Remember the saying, "All roads lead to Rome." That statement can be viewed from the perspective that all paths take us back to Oneness and eventually to our origin. Only you can choose how fast you want to get to that place of peace that is beyond human understanding. Remember when you hit a bump along the road, no matter how big or small, to call to mind the *neti, neti* principle from chapter two. You are only kissing frogs along your journey to the true Prince of peace.

Keep in mind that whatever changes you have decided to make to the words of your description or to your beliefs will take time to assimilate into your being. This is the case for most of us. Your choice to integrate changes into your life will be pretty strong if you have received guidance that dramatic changes need to be made in your core beliefs right away. Your choices, however, may fade a bit as time goes on. I implore you to review them occasionally as your awareness expands and you open to more light and love. Your writings can be used as inspiration on your soul's journey of illumination.

I feel the need to warn you again that the people who know you well may not appreciate the changes you are making as much as you do. Be compassionate toward them; they are unaware of the depth of your need to release beliefs that no longer serve your soul. I have found that as time goes on, our zeal for radical change mellows to a thoughtful and steady pace on our road to a truer self. You need not hold yourself to a standard of perfection, as that in itself can be destructive, but rather accept the Truth that you are made from the essence of unconditional love. Focus your efforts on removing the obstacles that get in the way of your unfolding to that higher Truth. You need to have compassion toward your humanness as well as compassion for others.

Follow the instructions in chapter four in regard to creating a ritual for any of the descriptive words or beliefs that no longer serve your soul and that you want to release.

≈

Renovating Your Sense of Self

You do not need anything outside your connection to the Truth of who you are. Everything else is an add-on to that core belief. Delightful as these things may be (and certainly there is no need to eliminate enjoyable experiences in the exterior world), the experiences and labels you give yourself are not an essential ingredient in building your self-esteem or your life. You improve your self-esteem by holding your higher ground and not compromising your beliefs or values to accommodate others, which would mean pulling yourself out of alignment and congruency. Dr. Terry Cole-Whittaker, an author and minister, titled one of her books: *What You Think of Me is None of My Business.* I love the sentiment that title carries. Receiving positive insight and input from those we trust is always helpful, but we should not absorb comments about who we are from those who judge us without truly knowing us. Be immune to words of fame and criticism by being centered in the Truth of who you are. Our sense of self must be centered on our connection to Spirit and to the Truth of who we are.

Each time you consciously waiver or allow yourself to succumb to another's beliefs, for whatever reason — fear of abandonment, humiliation, or just "going along" to fit in — you subvert your commitment to your true identity. That will always come with a cost to your identity. You sell a piece of yourself for a temporary moment in time that you perceived would bring you to a goal that will never be worth the price you paid: the betrayal of your true self. Episodes of betrayal chip away at your self-esteem because even though you may deny what happens to your soul, at some level within your inner being that deceit registers. Each betrayal begins a train of thought that weakens your power to stay centered in what you know to be true about yourself. You will begin to make excuses for the incongruent choices you have made.

A good clue that you may have compromised yourself is a nagging feeling that something is not quite right. When you become aware that your inner dialogue is arguing with itself and trying to rationalize why you did something, pay attention to that chatter. It is telling you that something is not right within. Reverently pray to have the core of the discontent revealed. Then use that knowledge to allow yourself to get back into alignment with Spirit.

GOING WITHIN: Just as the previous few sentences pointed out the value of paying attention to your inner dialogue to alert you to when you have compromised yourself, your inner dialogue, or self-talk, can often provide you with important information about how you value yourself. Spend a few moments to think about the message that is most frequently playing in your head. Is your inner dialogue one of self-degradation, unworthiness, and negativity? If it is, what do you think it is based on? Try to find the theme that runs through those messages. Once you can identify a theme, ask yourself how it fits into the Truth that you were created by Spirit. Think about what the congruencies are in those two aspects: your inner dialogue and the Truth of who you are. Are you having difficulty trying to find a common thread between them? Then try to identify the incongruities between your self-talk and the Truth of who you are. Was this an easier task to do? More than likely, it was.

This is a simple example of the conflict within our being. The conflict is similar to the grandfather's story about the two wolves in chapter four. The question remains, which wolf will you feed? As you know from reading that story, the choice is yours. Make sure you write about your interior dialogue; what you tell yourself about yourself and the incongruities between that talk and the Truth of who you are.

~

The Essence of Our True Selves

Eckhart Tolle teaches that the present moment, the Now, contains the essence of our true selves. His quote at the beginning of this chapter reflects that teaching: "To be still is to be conscious without thought. You are never more essentially, more deeply, yourself than when you are still." Many times events of our past are associated with guilt, while thoughts of our future are associated with fear. When you eliminate those thoughts about the past, you remove the associated guilt that event may have contained. Similarly, when you eliminate thoughts about the future, you remove the fear they may have contained and you are left with just the present. In the present moment, when you still your mind, you become aware of the subtle energy of your inner being. That peace and connection to your centered inner being are the anchors you can use to ground yourself when the waves of negativity begin to flow into your inner dialogue.

Can you really be anything other than the Presence that is in the Now, the Spirit you were created from? Do you think God made one mistake and that that one mistake is the flaw in the design that created you? Of course you know that is preposterous. What is true is that the negative self-talk you tell yourself is an illusion. Please understand, the illusion is your belief that your soul is "less than." Your self-talk is about your persona and not about your soul. So the way to get closer to your soul's peace is to eliminate what is not aligned with the essence of your soul. As you shift the quality of your self-talk, you will begin the process of untangling the untruths you have been telling yourself for years. Your inner dialogue will shift, and you will be more and more congruent with the Truth of who you are.

Going Within: Now let us examine the external dialogue you use. As always, humbly ask for the assistance of Divine grace to guide you through the process. Spend some time thinking about how you speak to others about yourself. Call to mind the exact words you use when describing yourself or the language you use to explain why you did something. Connect the choice of your language with the awareness that these words come from a belief you hold about yourself. How does this energy feel to you? Is it similar to your inner dialogue? Would you use this language to describe a dear and trusted friend? If not, you will see the problem immediately.

~

If it appears you do not hold yourself in the same high regard as a dear and trusted friend, you are living with someone, twenty-four seven, whom you do not hold in high regard.

Certainly this relationship with yourself needs improvement. You can begin to improve that relationship by closely monitoring your words and thoughts about yourself. Make a conscious decision to change your "story" about yourself. Push yourself to go deeply into reflection to find positive and loving aspects of yourself. Weave those aspects into your new story. That story could go something like, "I was created by Spirit, and I will build my soul's journey on the gifts I have been given by Spirit." Then fill in the rest of your story with positive things about yourself that you know to be true.

I know how difficult this can be. (Remember the story I told you about myself when I needed to write down positive things about myself? I truly struggled in trying to identify positive aspects about myself.) I also know that you can reach deeply inside yourself to create a different version of the same old tired story of how you are not good enough. As soon as you are able to put a few positive inputs together, feed the story to the good wolf and nurture the bad wolf since unconditional love nurtures all beings. This is the beginning of the renovation of your self-esteem.

Add to this renovation project the belief that you are a conduit for Spirit in the physical world and as such were provided unique gifts. Know that your soul continually evolves when you are aligned with the power that created you. To embrace this belief, you need to step out of the way of your narrow-sighted egoic mind and the illusion of separation. Once you begin to identify with the reality that because God created you, you are One with that creative force.

The renowned dancer Martha Graham has shared words of wisdom that speak to this connection with the creative power of the universe. She tells us that it is really not our business to decide how good or how valuable our creation is and not to compare it with others expressions. She instructs us to keep our channel open to the creative power of the universe, "period."

In the Hindu and Buddhist traditions, the word that describes our souls is *Atman,* the individual essence of God within your soul that is indistinguishable from God. In the Jewish and Christian traditions, this is described in scripture as being born in the image and likeness of God. With this belief firmly in your consciousness, it is not possible to become a victim unless you slide back into your identification of being separate from God. These are the beliefs from your higher consciousness usually associated with your interior world, but they are also the beliefs that are the underpinning of what shows up in the exterior world when you go out into the world to live your life.

Be sure to write about your interior and exterior dialogues. It will surprise you how quickly your dialogues will change when you focus on the new insights given to you. Check in periodically, jot down a few of the words from your new story, and note the progress on your journey. Create a ritual, if you choose, as you travel along, to release old stories as they leave you. Still, it may be worth keeping those old stories so you can check your progress and note any slipping back into your previous life.

Never Underestimate Who You Are

I recently became aware of a Greek named Epictetus who was born around 55 A.D. He was a Roman slave whose master was the secretary to Nero, the Roman emperor. Many years later, Epictetus was granted his freedom and began to teach philosophy in Rome. He traveled to Greece and became a philosopher and teacher and later founded a philosophical school in Greece. His central belief was that self-knowledge was essential in life.

Lao-tzu concurred with this teaching: "Knowing others is intelligence; knowing yourself is true wisdom. Mastering others is strength; mastering yourself is power." Socrates and Plato also concurred and taught the wisdom of "Know Thyself."

Epictetus also believed that what we see in others has more to do with who we are than with who other people are. He taught that we should use all conditions in life as practice to expand our knowledge of ourselves. His teachings are powerful reminders of the necessity to stay centered in the Truth of who we are.

The way we think about and perceive a challenge can contribute to our sense of a lack of power and control in a situation and create unwanted drama and chaos in our lives. We should never hold anyone else accountable for the judgment of a situation we choose to believe made us unhappy or angry. We need to hold only ourselves accountable. We should look at the situation itself and with discernment review our judgment and where our perspective has taken us. As you detach from your egoic mind's judgment, you create a space where you can be peaceful and centered. Observe your attachment when it happens, but remain as detached as possible emotionally, staying focused on your inner life rather than on your perspective of the spectacle of the challenge. Know that your mind's attachment to the challenge is the cause of your anger and frustration and can result in you becoming off center: losing your power, which results in your suffering.

This is a difficult practice to adhere to but is essential to not losing your alignment; this practice will allow you to avoid damaging your self-esteem and to remain connected to Spirit. This is a part of the path of surrendering to the present moment, a place of acceptance instead of resistance and "un-alignment" with the

Truth of who you are. Living purposefully from within instead of accidentally from without was one of the principal teachings of Raymond Charles Barker, a New Thought author and spiritual teacher. This teaching is wisdom you can use throughout your days to keep you on track toward your destination.

Going Within: This life you have been given is a blessed opportunity for you to find a union within to empower you so you can live the life that was intended for you, the life you were destined to have, and not the life of being disempowered by your exterior circumstances. Numerous books and movies have told the true stories of people who were born into wretched conditions and found the courage and strength within to rise above the limits that surrounded them. Epictetus was born a slave and ended his life as the founder of a school of philosophy. What makes you think you are any different? Seriously, how do you answer that question? Do not let yourself off the hook. Honestly give at least one answer to that question; your answer will expand your self-knowledge.

Make a list of the answers to the question, how are you different from people like Epictetus? Take a look at the list. Notice what you tell yourself about why you are not living the life you want to live. Write a feeling that is connected to each of the answers on your list and immerse yourself in the energy of that feeling. Now ask yourself whether those are the feelings you want to be the drivers of your life. If they are not, I suggest the following reflection.

Close your eyes and follow the path you have made to go within your being. Prepare yourself to receive answers to your questions. When you have arrived at that place within your soul that is now familiar to you, take each of your answers and the feeling connected to each, one by one, into your sacred place. Ask for Divine grace to reveal the underlying message that is there in your excuses to tell you why you cannot do the things you want to do to live the life you want. Ask for the support of Spirit to honor the answers by giving you the power to act on them. Write the revelations you were given in your journal. Repeat this process whenever you sense you are losing your center and you begin to feel "less than" in order to nurture your sense of self back to the Truth of who you are, Atman, not ego.

~

As you did previously, always be cognizant of your interior dialogue and the language you use when you refer to yourself externally to others. Add this discipline to your ongoing spiritual practice as you move forward on your soul journey to wholeness and alignment with the Truth of who you are. Remember that you do not have unconditional love, compassion, forgiveness, and reverence for all of life just for others. You need to include yourself in the practice. In fact, you are the most important person on whom to shower those blessings because, as many teachers have told us, you cannot give what you do not have.

I cannot emphasize enough the principle that our beliefs are the foundation of how we perceive the world within our being and the world that surrounds us. If we believe that we are unworthy of such blessings as love, happiness, and success, then the world we perceive within us will be how we perceive the external world, and this perception is what will be reflected back. When you build self-esteem and confidence in your alignment with Spirit, you will know when you are off track intuitively by how you feel. You can then go within and realign yourself. Joseph Campbell said: "The privilege of a lifetime is being who you are." When we identify who we are with our connection with Spirit, we are truly living our lives authentically.

As you shift the internal beliefs of who you are, the world around you has to shift to align with it because your beliefs have creative power, negative and positive. Remember that what you give your attention to and focus on will expand. Isaac Newton knew it was necessary to "keep the subject of my inquiry constantly before me and wait till the first dawning opens gradually, little by little into a full and clear light." This is the universal law of magnetic attraction. You have the power of that law to help you on your soul journey to wholeness. Also remember that in most cases this is a gradual process and requires that you "keep the subject of [your] inquiry constantly before [you]." To stop the never-ending flow of negative faultfinding of yourself, go within to the stillness of peace as soon as you are aware of its unsettling presence to find your connection to Source. It is also important to remember the core message of Mahatma Gandhi's powerful *Ahimsa* movement: to do no harm to any life form, which includes harming your own soul with degrading beliefs about yourself. Show reverence to your soul in all your choices of thoughts, words, and deeds directed to self and others.

The more we are able to build our self-esteem on the awareness of our connection to Spirit, the more confidence we will have that the answers we seek to life are within our being. The great masters have told us this. Their teachings have withstood the test of time. Buddha's devotees were distraught when they knew he was leaving his physical body and anxious about what would happen to them when he was no longer in the physical realm. He instructed them to "Be a light unto yourself."

These profound words of wisdom remind us to go deeply within ourselves to connect with the ever-present Divine, knowing that this is the place we can receive Divine grace and the guidance that will reveal to us the Truth of who we are. Christ taught this same Truth: "The kingdom of God is within." Saint John of the Cross framed it with his writings of receiving the *todo*, receiving God within by creating the *nada*. Kahlil Gibran, a Lebanese-American poet and author, told us that tenderness and kindness are not signs of weakness and despair, but manifestations of resolution and strength. All these highly evolved souls cannot be wrong. We need to follow their unified guidance. The more we trust and experience Spirit, the more we become aware that we are never alone, and fear begins to loosen its grip on our belief that we are not good enough. Our self-esteem, confidence, and self-respect soar, and our external world responds in kind. Spirit becomes our refuge and our strength.

I have found that as I have become more in alignment with the Truth of who I am, I am not creating nearly as many dramas in my life. This has become a profound shift in my life. Since birth, my life story has been pretty much an action-packed drama, one event following another, some of which I have shared with you. The change in the way I interact with the world around me has been remarkably noticeable, not only to myself but to those I am close to and who know me well. I now know beyond any doubt that the causative factors for these changes have been my intense search for self-knowledge, the amazing teachers I have been fortunate enough to be with, and the blessings of Divine grace that have guided me along the way on my soul journey.

If I had to pick just one thing that has had the most profound impact on this serious change of not creating drama in my life, it would certainly be the undeniable awareness that I am never alone and that I have nothing to fear when I am connected to the Divine and open to the flow of Divine grace and guidance. I no longer search outside myself for wholeness; my focus has shifted to going within. Because of this inner connection to the Divine, I am much more able to enjoy the amazing world around me, the enormous blessings of family and friends, the beauty of the world I live in, and the abundance in my life. I am thankful for all that I have been blessed with and look forward to all that is yet to come.

I leave you in this chapter with one of St. Teresa of Avila's prayers that captures the sentiment of Spirit becoming your refuge and your strength:

Let nothing disturb you.
Let nothing make you afraid.
All things are passing.
God alone never changes.
Patience gains all things.
If you have God, you will want for nothing.
God alone suffices.

Bring the feelings that these most reverent words evoke within you and the wisdom you have gained from your reflections revealed by Divine grace to the continuation of your soul's journey in the next two chapters as you stay the course in your journey in the exterior world.

CHAPTER 7

RELEASING THE DAM OF SEPARATION WITH THE FLOW OF DIVINE GRACE:

THE SACRAL CHAKRA

The survival fears of our sacral chakra are being soothed by the unstoppable love of Divine grace as it washes over our sense of being alone in this worldly experience. We are awakening to the power of the current that is moving debris, boulders, this rubble of the broken dreams and disappointments of our constricted past.

Gratitude is what we are without a story.
— *Byron Katie*

When I despair, I remember that all through history,
the ways of truth and love have always won.
— *Mahatma Gandhi*

THE ENERGY OF THE SACRAL CHAKRA guides how we perceive and engage with the physical world around us. Illusion here has a strong element of reality because we are in the realm of time, space, and form. Yet viewing the physical world from the perspective of your higher consciousness will help you to maintain your alignment. Remember what St. Teresa encouraged us to do, to see God in the details of our days. The focus is on surviving in our environment, as well as on one-on-one relationships, sensuality, and our ability to connect with the creative energy of the universe.

In the last chapter my focus was on our sense of self, our self-esteem in this world. In this chapter we explore how we sense the "other" in a relationship in our physical world. Many authors through the years connect this chakra with the sexual organs because of its position in the sacral area of the human body, the prostrate in the male and the uterus in the female. This can be viewed as opposing energies, female and male, putting us in the world of duality. When these opposing energies are in an integrated flow like the *yin yang*, it is the coming together of the sperm and the egg in the creation of new life as one. Christine Page, M.D., the author of *Spiritual Alchemy*, writes in her book that the "spiritual quality available in this area is respect, where every relationship is sacred and hence the name," sacral chakra. We will explore different aspects of the sacral chakra energies: our survival reactions, our sensuality, and our creativity.

CONTAINING FIGHT OR FLIGHT REACTIONS

Our powerful "fight or flight" survival reaction is one of the strongest instincts we carry in the depths of our psyche. It is a reaction that has great influence over how we interact with our physical world. This instinct has always been in the human psyche. In prehistoric times, it served us when we were confronted by predators that had the potential to end our lives. We have carried this behavioral pattern into present times, and it still figures in our automatic responses to perceived danger: physically, emotionally, and behaviorally. When we are not connected to Spirit, our behavior may become angry or aggressive if we think someone is a threat to our well-being, physically or emotionally. We may become withdrawn and isolate ourselves if we do not have an appropriate response to the threat, or we may escape into an addictive behavior pattern to any number of things, to work, substances, exercise, or overeating, for example, in an effort to calm ourselves.

This reaction is rooted in the way most of us perceive our physical world today: with a deep sense of being alone. This drive for survival that many of us carry, of "me" against "you," can color all our interactions with our physical environment. The focus of self-survival is so ingrained in us that it has a profound effect on how we live our lives. When we are trapped in this perception all our one-on-one relationships are less than satisfying because of the protective barriers we put up and the inability to allow ourselves to be intimately vulnerable with anyone. Our physical senses are dulled to the enormous beauty in the world that surrounds us. These barriers also prevent our ability to let Divine creativity flow through us and be manifest in our physical world. Let us explore each of these areas of our lives, our survival reaction, our sensuality, and our creativity, from the viewpoint of the sacral chakra.

Our survival instinct has the ability to magnify our fear of not having what we need to "get by" in this world and, obviously, can be very ego driven. The instinct can be toward anything from such basic needs as food, money, and housing to the need to connect with another person in a personal way. It touches, for example, on our sense of the personal power we have in our work endeavors and our relationships as well as on our ability to take care of our nonphysical needs. This sense of feeling inferior can paralyze us, which often results in being fearful of being seen as weak and easily controlled. Such fears can easily overwhelm us and many times bind us to inaction. We again confirm our sense of being "less than" in the world when we do not take action, and a destructive pattern is thereby reinforced.

Other times, because of our fears and a lack of trust, we attempt to control or manipulate circumstances, people, and our environment, or we move into an avoidance mode of behavior. We may even resort to flattery or charming another person in an effort to catch them off guard so we can manipulate a situation to our benefit. Trying to make the other feel guilty is yet another means of manipulating or controlling a situation. Any way we approach the need to manipulate and control a situation with someone or to control another person in an attempt to control their power draws us away from the Truth of who we are.

Many times, we come from a place of trying to control others from a fear they will usurp our power in a particular situation. This impulse can be based in the false belief that we know what is best. We take charge, intervening to improve a situation to benefit those involved. How many times have we found ourselves in a situation where we were trying to "fix" it and instead, it blew up? Then our feeble response is "I was only trying to help" instead of being authentic and "owning" our desire to control the situation. When we are motivated by fear and consequently feel the need to control our surroundings, that energy drives our attempts to "help," and the results are usually disastrous.

GOING WITHIN: Take a few moments here to reflect on a situation with someone when you knew you were dead-on right, and yet the result was far less than what you had expected. You had convinced yourself that for the good of all you would step up to the plate and take control because you felt the situation was going in the wrong direction. What was the motivating factor that drove your action? Was it a need for manipulation or power, or was it a need to compete? Did it give you a sense of superiority because you "knew" you were right? Did you feel a sense of "If I don't do it, who will?" or an overwhelming sense of responsibility? Go within, and really make an effort to find the motivating factor of why you took action. It is really important that you search for an authentic answer to this inquiry. Be open to any answer that comes to you from within. Do not discount it if it does not resonate with you at first. Contemplate the answer and be open to its guidance before deciding it is of no value to your soul.

We usually do not want to hear that we have had less than good intentions when we move into action, but this is crucial to knowing what drives us to do the things we do. This underlying motivator is more than likely a prevalent part of our psyche, one that may be unconscious. Spend as much time as you need here to really grasp what that force is. As with all the other contemplative reflections you have done, reverently pray for Divine grace to reveal to you what the force is behind your actions in these situations. Write down all the answers that come to you, whether or not you agree with them. Then spend a few days with the ones you rejected outright, asking for insight as to why you rejected them so strongly. Remember the words from Shakespeare's *Hamlet*, "The lady doth protest too much, methinks." Humbly ask in prayer for the courage to open yourself to the shadow energies that lurk within you.

Once you have been able to identify your motivating factor or factors, relive the experience with the realization that your judgment proved to be not only wrong but entirely clouded by your perspective of the event and by your need to take control and be powerful. This should be a real learning experience for you. Maybe you were left with a feeling of confusion as a result of being unconscious of your motivation and that you had failed (the key word being *failed*) in your attempt to improve the situation, though you had no idea where you went wrong. Remember Bernie Siegel's belief about failure, "F is not for failure but for feedback." Every experience we have has a component of soul growth, be it interpreted as negative or positive by us.

Retrospectively, look at that situation as a spiritual alchemist, searching for the golden wisdom in the apparent lead that the situation contained for you. The wisdom you receive may be as simple as knowing what *not* to do the next time, because what you did this time did not work out, similar to, "Well, I won't do that again." This fits into the *neti, neti* principle of elimination that shows up on the journey of illumination fairly frequently. Or the wisdom you receive may be the revelation of a behavior that you have used in your life for a long time, unconscious of it. You may have looked back on situations and wondered why things turned out as they still do so often. You are left feeling exasperated and find yourself saying, "Why does this always happen to me?" Or "I cannot believe this happened again!" The insight you have received may be the piece of information about yourself that may be the answer to those types of questions for you.

≈

THE GIFTS OF RELATIONSHIPS

Living in a body on earth makes it almost impossible to go through life without encountering challenges, especially in our relationships with others, no matter what type of relationship it is, from personal to business. This earth, this place of manifested form, provides us with plenty of opportunities for growth and expansion, even when we are not consciously interested. Some of us have taken great pains *not* to be in relationships and have closed our hearts. Unfortunately, we have cut ourselves off from experiences that relationships offer, and they do offer a rich field to grow in. The beautiful lotus flower offers a great analogy of the growth that is available to us when we are open to life's hidden gifts. The lotus blossom is exquisite, though when we are looking only at its surface, we do not see from whence it came. This magnificent flower had to grow out of mud below the dark and murky waters of a pond, which was therefore responsible for its magnificence. Its focus never strayed from reaching for the light. We can view our lives in this way and remember to keep our focus on the light instead of the darkness that we find ourselves in along the way. Strive to see the world within and without through the vision of the Beloved, seeing Spirit in all things.

Relationships are among the most valuable tools we have for looking at ourselves, whether we want to or not, especially in one-on-one relationships. They can be the very mirrors we need to see our true reflection. Sathya Sai Baba said that one of the best ways to rid ourselves of our ego is to get married. When my husband and I were fortunate enough to have an interview with Sathya Sai Baba, the first thing he asked us, in perfect English, was, "So how's the fighting going?" and laughed and laughed. It was not until years later that I had any true understanding of what he was directing us to look at.

The interactions between two people have the potential of bringing out the best and worst in us. From a more conscious perspective, the "worst" is just as valuable and many times more valuable than our best behavior in gaining self-knowledge.

The worst in us can contain hidden gems that can illuminate the dilemmas we find ourselves in. For instance, "I can't believe I keep getting sucked into this kind of argument!" and "Why does that person always bring out the worst in me?" or "I can't believe I said that to this person! What's up with that?" These are soul-searching questions that go to the core of our fears of not being able to survive on our own. They need to be asked from that sacred place within, with an open heart, listening for the answers we need to guide us in how to have successful relationships.

Namaste, a Sanskrit word, is one way to think of "the other" in one-on-one relationships. It helps us to remain heart focused in our interactions. It is a word of greeting that is usually accompanied by a physical gesture: palms together placed over the heart or the palms together with the fingertips touching the forehead with a gentle bow. One meaning of *Namaste* is: the Divinity in me bows to the Divinity in you. This reminds us of the Oneness aspect of each of us. It shifts our energy to respecting one another and opens a space of true communication, that of heart to heart.

Caroline Myss gave a workshop in Arizona where she lectured on how to be a congruent person — no small task, to say the least. She explained her method of teaching the chakra system and drew a diagram of the chakras in a three-column format on her whiteboard, as she had many times before in workshops. The first column represents our physical world, the second our interior world, and the third, the cosmic realm. She writes numbers in each column to represent each chakra and to describe the realm of influence that particular chakra has. I am familiar with this format, as I have studied with Myss for years, but this time, something really caught my eye.

She teaches a ten-chakra system. In the first column of her diagram, next to the number 2, representing the sacral chakra, she wrote "1–1" to symbolize that the sacral chakra is associated with our one-on-one relationships, be they personal or business relationships. When I saw the 2 followed by "1–1," I immediately thought of 211, the "Info Line" phone number. It is a phone referral service that provides information about all the social services in my home state of Connecticut. In that moment, it symbolized to me all the information and feedback we get from our "1–1" relationships.

Can our "1–1" power struggles not be viewed as a virtual school that provides us with an enormous amount of information to use to obtain a clearer vision of how our egoic mind perceives our interactions? Do not our one-on-one relationships provide us with constant input on where we need to open to Divine guidance and grace to reveal where and how we need to grow? This visual of 2-1-1 deepened my appreciation of the challenges and opportunities for growth that one-on-one relationships provide as I encounter them in my daily life.

Many times when I am conscious enough, I am able to view the challenging or life-affirming situations I encounter in my relationships as essential "information" that I am being given to assist me on my soul's journey of illumination. In regard to the challenges that "show up" in life, some of the people who appear can be master teachers, the *noble adversaries* I wrote about previously. I know from experience that these souls have come into my life to teach me powerful and invaluable wisdom to help me to move forward on my path of illumination. I am also struck with a sense of awe when I become aware, in retrospect, of how these *noble adversaries* appeared in my life, through the power of Divine synchronicity.

We have been given the gift of life, and life provides us with innumerable learning opportunities, experiences, and teachers that are God's instruments in providing us with the information necessary for our soul's expansion. Ask that your reactionary instinctual responses to life's challenges be infused with Divine grace so you may gain the wisdom they have to offer. Know that you can bring unconditional love to your relationships, instead of inserting the negative energy of controlling power, to change the vibrational frequency of a challenge you may confront.

Continually remind yourself of your own life experiences, those that occurred when you knew you were connected to the Divine because of the way those challenges unfolded. This will reinforce your belief that you will not be facing challenges in your future alone. When we open ourselves to the wisdom these events reveal, we will move farther along on our way to our Source. Our world is continually giving us information that we can use to guide us on our journey, if only we have the insight to recognize it. Now when I am conscious enough to be aware of the gift that the current situation is giving me, whether challenging or life affirming, I think: 211. This is information I need.

In every one-on-one relationship obviously there are two people, and therefore there are two perspectives of how the relationship is providing valuable information. Just as we receive information from the other in our relationship, the other is receiving information from us. The information each receives, however, is not the information the other may have intended to give. Remember what Epictetus told us: what we see in others has more to do with us than with who the other people are. The information always needs to go through our filters and is processed according to our listening capabilities and how centered we are. This awareness should give us pause. Take the opportunity to reflect on this; ask yourself how you process the information you receive. If it is inaccurate, is it inaccurate because of the filters you put on it or because it is reflecting who you are rather than what the other is trying to relate to you? The next time someone tells you that what he or she said was not what you heard, take that within and search for how you might be misinterpreting the message.

In a recently released documentary called *Wake Up*, Jonas Elrod, a filmmaker and the director of *Wake Up*, started "seeing" things overnight. In an interview with Oprah Winfrey, Elrod shared that overnight he began seeing auras, energies in geometric forms, spirits, demons, and angels. He searched out many different spiritual teachers and scientists in an effort to determine what he was seeing and why. One of the spiritual teachers he sought out was Abdi Assadhi, a spiritual healer, acupuncturist and the author of *Shadows on the Path*, who practices in New York.

In one of their encounters, Elrod asks Assadhi for other spiritual practices besides meditation, which he finds useful, to help him on his journey. Assadhi responds, "So you're looking for spiritual things? Be in a relationship with your girl [Elrod has been in a longtime relationship]. I always say it is the deepest thing; it is the most difficult thing. Not to lie in it, not to hide in it, to be conscious in it. It is more than romantic love. It is about being naked in front of another human being so you can see yourself naked. The mirroring helps you to see. It is kind of hard to see if you do not have a mirror. If I do not have a mirror, I do not know what I look like. Relationship is that. So if you want spirituality, you have it right in front of you. That is the big trick. You get comfortable in that and the rest will follow."

Elizabeth Gilbert tells us that we think a soul mate is a perfect fit. She explains that a true soul mate is someone who mirrors back to you the things you need to change on your spiritual journey that will ultimately change your life.

Spend some time reviewing the way you interact with other people, not just the relationship you have with a partner. As you go about your day, be mindful of the type of energy emanating from your being as you pass others along the way. Keep in mind that there are more ways to communicate with someone than with words. After reading the next paragraph regarding scientific research on this subject, you are likely to give serious thought to the kind of energy you are sending out into your world and how you go about sending it.

This is from another article about Newberg and Waldman, the neuroscience researchers mentioned in chapters four and five, titled "God and the Neuroscientific," in which they describe how our brain neurons resonate with the facial expressions, body language, and tone of voice of the person with whom we are interacting. They explain that when we engage with a person who is emanating peaceful energy, our brain reacts in a similar way. "Neurochemicals that stimulate bonds of friendship and intimacy are released, and when this occurs, we become more socially cooperative, responding with generosity, compassion, and fairness." They go on to describe how, when the person we are interacting with changes his or her expression to one of anger, for example, our old reptilian limbic system automatically kicks into the fight-or-flight reaction of survival. The authors include brain scan images to demonstrate the brain activity that takes place in response to our perspective of a situation in which we are engaged.

WE ARE NEVER ALONE

As I have said many times before here, we are never, ever alone, but we do need to take the initiative in being open to the Divine communicating with us. This is the one-on-one relationship that we can always trust to be there for us. Like all relationships, we need to develop a connection with it. We need to attune to the "language" of the Divine so we know what is being communicated to us. By this I do not mean literal language but the essence of the communication. My experience of this is more in the realm of "knowing" than in hearing actual words when I am communicating with the Divine, although there have been times when the communication has been emphatic and clear words were given. Actually, this book is the result of clear words I received: "Write this."

Sometimes a thought comes into my mind that is exact, perfect for the situation I am in, and I am very aware that it did not come from me. It comes not just when I am struggling but also when I should reach out and touch someone with love. As this communication grows, fearful survival reactions will recede because you "know" you are never alone when you have developed a bond with the Divine in this relationship. Whenever you are frightened and need help, remember St. Teresa's words: "If you have God, you will want for nothing. God alone suffices."

Another aspect to take into all your one-on-one relationships is the awareness that the other person in this relationship is a manifestation of Spirit just as you are. The other has a soul and a soul journey that they are traveling on, just as you are. The more we can hold that awareness in our heart, we will interact with that person with compassion and reverence for his or her soul even when we are disagreeing or on the opposite end of that person's core beliefs. When we are on opposite ends of the spectrum, this should not be the focus of the interaction. The awareness should be focused on honoring the God within them who happens to believe and act differently than I do. This is a difficult consciousness to hold when we are being attacked in some way, but in the long run it is the only way to honor God and ourselves. This is the value of *Ahimsa*, nonviolence toward every form of life. Therefore, do no harm to the other's soul or to your soul, as we are both in God's creation of Oneness.

All our relationships, be they family, friend, or sexual relationships, offer an opportunity for soul growth and the potential to provide the information we need to address difficult issues, from how to share finances with someone to possible shame regarding our sexuality. Shame is an extraordinarily powerful negative energy that can drain our ability to connect with others and with the Divine. It is imperative that we understand that there is nothing we can do to put us in a position of not being unconditionally loved by the Divine.

There is a parable in Christian scripture that addresses the issue of a son whose behavior was less than stellar, called the parable of the Prodigal Son. It is a parable that Christ told his followers about a father who had two sons. The younger of his two sons asked that his inheritance be given to him now instead of waiting until his father's death. The father agreed and gave the inheritance to this son, who then proceeded to go out into the world and make his own way. He lived a wild life and eventually was not able to take care of himself, when a drought hit the area where he lived. He ended up in a menial job and realized he would be better off at his father's home working for him. This son was able to go beyond his shame and seek his father's forgiveness. His father rejoiced in his return and compared this son to having been dead and then being alive, lost but now found. The father's joyful reception of his son is an illustration of God's unconditional love for each of us.

SENSUALITY

As I mentioned at the beginning of this chapter, the sacral chakra is associated with the sexual organs because of the chakra's anatomical proximity to the female and male organs and, like *yin yang*, we hold both of the energies that we associate with female and male characteristics. When we are able to integrate these powerful complementary energies, sometimes described as passive and aggressive, in a more positive light, such as receiving and giving, and in a loving way, our relationships are compatible and rewarding. Even though these forces appear to be polar opposites, they are quite interdependent in our exterior physical world, and we need to integrate them in that way in our internal world in order to bring our full self into our personal relationships.

We can experience the energies in our internal world, in our minds and emotions, as well as our physical body. When balanced, the interplay of energies lends a cohesive fuel to personal relationships. We are able to accept times of dependence and independence in a healthy relationship as the ebb and flow of the energies move and shift for both sexes without fear. This is the same for same-sex relationships. The integration of energies also allows us to be more open to intimacy and vulnerability with our partner and ourselves. When relationships become tainted with power struggles and manipulative maneuvers, the natural flow of the relationship is restricted and can become abusive and threatening. This can result in the inability of one or both people in the relationship to receive the love offered by the other, and each will reject the other's advances toward reconciliation if a balance of the energies is not restored to a harmonious flow.

Our five senses are another medium for experiencing the essence of the Divine. I have already written about the feeling of awe when we visually witness a magnificent sunrise painted by Spirit in the sky for all who care to partake in its majesty. The admission price is opening your soul to beauty beyond comprehension. My husband and I were blessed with the opportunity to make a four-month cross-country road trip from Connecticut to California, up through Canada and into Alaska. I cannot begin to describe the majestic grandeur of nature that we experienced. The vistas took my breath away, and try as hard as I could, I could not take them fully within because they were too immense, humbling beyond words. These experiences of nature make me realize how infinitesimally small we are in the grand scheme of creation. The night sky, where I could see more stars than I had ever seen before, drew my consciousness to a world beyond my imagination.

On a much smaller scale, I am sure you have bitten into a luscious piece of fruit and the taste of it made you pause for just a second to take in the perfect flavor, uttering internally, "Oh my, that's really, really good." That taste is a creation of Spirit. How about the sounds of water, birds, or music that touch your soul and give you pause, a still stirring within your being. Those soothing sounds are creations of Spirit. Then there is the smell of the earth, rich and organic, or the aromatic fragrance of an exquisite flower; these too are the creations of Spirit. The last sense I want to touch on is touch, the gentle caress of a breeze against your cheek, the smoothness of moss beneath your feet in the forest, or the tender, warm touch of your beloved. Again, these are creations of Spirit. I am sure you can add an enormous list of sensual pleasures to my few examples. All of them can take you to a place of connection with Spirit and give you another way to experience God in the details of your ordinary days. You can choose to experience creation from whatever senses you have been blessed with.

INSPIRED CREATIVITY

The sacral chakra is also strongly related to the power of creativity, by which I mean our ability to bring forth into the physical world the inspirational ideas we receive from the Divine or even the changes we consciously make within ourselves. "To exist is to change, to change is to mature, to mature is to go on creating myself endlessly." These are the words that Henri Bergson, French philosopher and Nobel Laureate in literature, used to describe creativity within himself. We all have been inspired by a wondrous thought or sight that moves our very beings. I choose to refer to that inspirational moment as a moment of being touched by the Divine.

It is that instant when the veil is lifted from our very souls, and we have a sense of Spirit, that indescribable awareness deep within our beings that comes with bliss, joy, peace, and awe. We may question where the gift comes from, but there is no doubt that we have been given a precious moment of a glimpse of the Divine.

We may receive a brilliant insight into how to resolve an issue we have been struggling with for years or an original idea of how to solve a problem that has been in the current events of our time. We may be inspired to try to capture our experience by depicting it in a painting or in a song. The question then becomes, do we have the capacity to manifest the message into physical form and incorporate it into our lives and the lives of others? Do we have the courage to be a cooperative part of bringing an inspiration we have received into the realm of the physical world? Neil Donald Walsh, an author and spiritual teacher tells us that creativity is not something you wait for. It is something that is waiting for you.

Creation is usually referred to as something that has happened in the past, as the beginning of the universe, something that has already happened. But creation is an ongoing process, an active energy that never stops creating. We can open ourselves to it and manifest something wondrous in the world consciously, or allow that portion of creativity we receive, by default, to create unconsciously something less than wondrous, something we have not committed our whole selves to. I read once that in order to fulfill a Divine expression, God plants an idea in your heart. Is it time for you to use your creativity to bring that Divine expression into form? Reflect on the possibility of doing that. Uncover what the barriers are that stand in your way. By "barriers," I mean the excuses that you tell yourself as to why you could not possibly give birth to a creative idea you have been given. Do not make the mistake of leaving this earth with a Divine expression you have been given still in your heart and not in the world.

Thomas Merton, a Trappist monk, social activist, and prolific spiritual author shares with us that he believes that creativity is creating something for our very soul out of every experience in our own ordinary life. These words of wisdom should help us understand that the events in our lives are really gifts for our growth. As we go through our days, we are continually creating new thoughts and ideas that affect our "reality." Our interactions with others and their realities can have a strong influence on our creativity as ours can on theirs. By surrounding ourselves with people who lift us up, encourage us, and support us in our endeavors to be our best and as we do for them, we are nurturing our ability to create a loving and compassionate world around us. These supportive people allow our creative impulses and dreams to expand.

Psychologists have called the influence of these supportive people in our lives the Michelangelo Phenomenon. Stephen Drigotas, Ph.D., a psychology professor at John Hopkins University, tells that through a largely unconscious process, confidence and belief in each other's abilities can effect each other in a way that can bring us to our highest potential. These reassuring relationships contribute to our sense of self, our creativity, and help to "sculpt" us to be the best that we can envision for others and ourselves.

My limited understanding of what allowed for the creative inspiration I received for this book has to do with the process of creating that space within myself for Spirit to enter. As I reflect on each time I have received a gift of inspiration that is undoubtedly from Spirit, I recall that I had been in a space of inner peace. It was not during a prayer time of requesting something. Rather it was during a time of appreciation for all my blessings and for the awareness of being watched over each day of my life, the great days and the horrid days that have brought me to the place I am in now. As a child I had a sense of this protection, but as my life progressed, like most of us, I was drawn out into the world of alluring illusion and became trapped in my ego identification of what little connection to God I had created space for.

Fear and control were the real driving forces for me throughout most of my life, yet I was always aware of God in my life,
even though the screaming of fear almost deafened my ability to hear Spirit's presence. Although I say that, I think that is
why St. John of the Cross's description of creating the *nada* for
God to enter hit me like a missile that morning I was reading
about him. At the time I knew that whatever I was experiencing
was huge, but I was not conscious of what it was. I now think
that my awareness of the need to go deeply within my being to
find the peace of God so many years ago created the space that
allowed me to receive inspiration. Then, I had no awareness of
how essential that is to receiving God. Though I was filled with
awe and profoundly moved by what happened to me that morning while reading about St. John, I was unaware that there was
space in my being to receive such a gift. At this point in my life
I am no longer driven by a need to know why things happen
as they do. I seem to have shifted into surrendering that need
and have gone beyond reason. That has allowed me to create
more space within. Campbell tells us that "awe is what moves
us forward."

I struggled with my own sense of not being good enough
when I received inspiration for this book. The power of the
experience that inspired this book was something too strong
for me to deny; it was something beyond my ability to imagine.
Somewhere deep within my being I knew that if I did not take
the plunge and bring my experience into the physical world that
I would regret it for the rest of my life and take that regret to
my grave.

The energy of not following through on this gift would have
been like a continual, insidious undermining of my soul. I had
to come to terms with the internal voices of doubt sounding in

my mind. With courage that was infused with Divine grace, I walked into the "who do you think you are" bells that rang. I knew I had to honor the gift for myself and not for anyone else. I needed to stay focused on the gift and not the outcome. The feeling I have about the outcome of this gift is like the story I shared previously about the farmer whose stallion ran away and whose neighbor thought it was a bad thing. The farmer took the experience, as "we will see." I am more than blessed by having received the gift and the process of birthing it into physical form. That alone is truly more than enough. I hope sharing my sense of inadequacy about writing a book, as well as about Divine grace, will help you to bring into the world a creative gift that you carry in your heart. Please share it with others.

≈

I am sure you have experienced similar illuminating moments, and I imagine there are many more than you could possibly count or remember. Ralph Waldo Emerson told us that "a man should learn to detect and watch that gleam of light which flashes across his mind from within." Were your moments of inspiration like a soft whisper that you could not quite latch on to, or like the flashes of light that Emerson refers to? However inspiration comes to you, you intuitively know you have been touched by something deep within you. I strongly encourage you to honor those moments by whatever you feel inspired to do. Do not let them slip away into the "busy-ness" of your life. The more you honor those precious moments, the more open you will be to receiving more inspiration. If you have received inspiration to create something specific and do not, it can drain your self-esteem. More important, it can be a drain on your soul because you will have sabotaged yourself. You will have compromised a gift from the Divine, which will be a heavy awareness to carry in your soul.

I have found that the more I pay attention, acknowledge, create the space to receive inspiration, and align myself with occurrences of inspiration, the more I am able to incorporate such experiences into my consciousness. As we drink in the restorative energy that we have come to recognize as Divine grace and the blessings it carries, we become aware of how much we, as individuals, are capable of and are changing.

By virtue of our focused efforts in releasing the resistance and debris that fear created in our beliefs, we have created more and more of the space that St. John of the Cross described as *nada,* intentionally creating the space to receive inspiration. This is usually a gradual process of creating a vessel to receive the flow of Divine grace so we can receive the *todo* St. John referred to. The more we are able to hold ourselves open to the powerful force and not let our egoic minds and fear slip in, the more we manifest the blessings in the physical world. We find ourselves becoming more unconditionally loving and compassionate. We also become aware that we are unfolding into what Neil Diamond wrote about in his song "Be" from his album *Jonathon Livingston Seagull* so many years ago. Here are a few lines of the lyrics:

Be
As a page that aches for a word
Which speaks on a theme that is timeless
While the Sun God will make for your way

We, through the power of Divine grace, will become the pages that Creator will write on. Divine grace will transform the creative inspirations we receive from Spirit into our physical world without attachment to the outcome. Divine grace transforms our creative abilities into manifested form. We will be the flutes on which Creator will play the most harmonious melodies. We will be the observers of this magnificent gift of life as we travel on our soul's journey of illumination.

As we move to the next chapter, hold the awareness of the "other and you" as one in the Oneness of creation that Divine grace revealed to you. We will need to expand that awareness to include many, many more souls.

CHAPTER 8

OPENING THE FLOODGATES OF ONENESS BY EMBRACING DIVINE GRACE:
THE ROOT CHAKRA

The current of this cleansing force is now a powerful waterfall. It crashes down on the things that impede its flow and has its way with our doubts, judgments, and constrictions of our root chakra. It breaks through the barriers of our limited sense of self. It overflows the banks of our limited vision of life and floods our experience of life with the stunning mystical experience of living life as it was intended!

That which is Below corresponds to that which is Above, and that which is Above corresponds to that which is Below, to accomplish the miracles of the One Thing."
— *Hermes Emerald Tablet*

Quantum physics thus reveals a basic oneness of the universe.
— *Erwin Schrodinger*

THE ROOT CHAKRA, sometimes referred to as the base chakra, is located at the base of our spine, the place where we touch the earth when we sit. It is the energy center where we ground ourselves to the physical world. We also ground ourselves by building a strong foundation of beliefs that keeps our energies centered and in present time and ourselves solidly united with our convictions. As I noted before, we develop our beliefs first from the environment of our immediate family and then expand to our extended family, the community, the country, and then to the world community, the solar system, and ultimately to the universe. In the world we live in today, we have access to information that goes well beyond what humanity was aware of a short time ago. As a result of the explosion of technology, our world has stretched as far as our telescopes can detect, far beyond our solar system. The Internet has truly made us a global village. Information from cyberspace affects how we view our world, what we believe about it, and our role in it, from a basic tribal connection to a connection with the cosmos. Let us begin with our first tribal beliefs and work our way to cosmic beliefs.

BEING PRESENT

One way of describing being grounded is the practice of being mindful in whatever you are doing in the present moment. Many times, instead of being present, we are not present or even sure of where we are. We are unconscious of the present moment because we are wandering somewhere else in our minds. We can learn from the past, but it is essential that we live in the present. I am sure you have had the experience of driving somewhere, especially if to somewhere you drive regularly, arriving at your destination, and you cannot remember how you came there. A part of your mind and the energy it contains were somewhere else and not in the present moment.

When our energies are scattered, we are not focused or single-minded and will not be able to manifest our aspirations in the physical world. This can be as simple as deciding to go to the store, being distracted by something, and never accomplishing our original task. Imagine how your life would be if this were a more common occurrence than not, what a day in your life would be like if your energies were scattered for most of the day. You can see that not only would you not achieve what you wanted, but you would probably be frustrated and, what is more likely, the people around you would be frustrated as well, especially if they are counting on you to do something.

I have given an example of what not being present does to us when I told you about retrieving the fragments of our being that were still captured in our past, which was Caroline Myss's first homework assignment in her mysticism class. Many times the lack of being present allows others to have more influence over us than is healthy, and we may take on beliefs that are not those we would choose had we been fully present within ourselves.

Being present to the moment is so important that it is the first step in the Buddhist teachings of the Seven Factors of the Path to Enlightenment:

1. Mindfulness: Being in the Now, the present moment

2. Investigation: Discernment and searching for the Truth

3. Energy: Perseverance in your search for the Truth

4. Joy: The state of mental quietude and stillness

5. Tranquility: The state of serenity in body and mind

6. Concentration: Perpetual and abiding one-pointedness

7. Equanimity: The state of equipoise, nonreaction to the fluctuations or spectacles of life

In the clinical world of psychology, the therapeutic effect of mindfulness has been shown to provide beneficial results in the mentation (or mental activity) of clients, so much so that some clinical therapists have incorporated mindfulness practices in the treatment plan of their clients since the 1970s. The aspect of being able to provide clients with a means to control, or self-regulate, their minds — and therefore their actions — to external or internal stimulus results in a significant self-empowering effect and contributes to the stability of the client's life.

Mindfulness can really be a transformational approach to how you perceive your surroundings and your life. It requires that you self-regulate your attention and become consciously aware of what is happening in the present moment, both in your interior and exterior world. Mindfulness gives us the power to be detached observers of the external world and all its capricious and vacillating dramas in the present moment.

Do you remember the story I related in chapter four about the Chinese farmer whose neighbor rushed over when he heard about the Chinese farmer's prize stallion running away? The neighbor returned when the stallion came back with others horses and again when his son was thrown off one of the new horses and broke his leg. Do you remember the farmer's response to his neighbor? On each occasion it was "We'll see." His response was one of detached observation of his external world in the present moment. The neighbor's response reflected a state of continual reaction to the spectacles of life.

GOING WITHIN: Close your eyes and think about where your mind has been for at least the past hour. Even though you might have been reading this book for some of that time, has your full attention been focused on each word you have read? Did you find yourself needing to reread something because your mind had drifted to some other place? Did your mind drift to a meeting that you attended and to what took place there? Did you start to think about something that you need to do tomorrow? Take a few minutes now to write down in your journal all the things you can recall that your mind drifted to that caused you not to be present in reading this book or the moment of any other activity of the past hour. Look at the places you have gone instead of being in the present. Use this awareness to realize how many places you go other than the present moment on a regular basis. This awareness will help you recognize when you drift away from being present, thus unable to capture precious moments of sacred experiences or knowings.

~

Another amazing outcome of being mindful of the present moment is what is referred to as the Beginner's Mind: having the ability to look at something as though you are seeing or experiencing it for the first time. The Beginner's Mind approaches life with the innocence of first queries into what is. The practice of being in the present moment requires that we come to the present with no judgments or opinions, leaving us open to anything as a possibility. In chapter seven I told you about the experience of the majestic vistas in nature on my cross-country trip, but what I was not aware of was the effect that would have on how I looked at the area where I live.

For more than thirty-five years I have been fortunate to live in a fairly rural area close to a huge reservoir. I frequently walk along the reservoir trail and thoroughly enjoy its beauty. I was not prepared for what happened on my first walk there upon returning from my cross-country trip. It was as though I were seeing and experiencing the trail for the first time. My mind was having a hard time comprehending what was going on. The experience of being fully present in the moment while in the majesty of nature on that trip had opened a space within my being, changing something within me; it had given me the blessing of seeing things with the purity of a Beginner's Mind.

Tribal Beliefs

As I have said, we have beliefs about everything we do, and those beliefs set the ground rules for how we can influence our own lives. When we first arrive in the world in the physical form, we need to develop a set of beliefs that will determine how we manage our energies, or powers, and therefore our lives. Most of us begin our life journey saturated with tribal beliefs that are difficult to release. These and our surroundings have an enormous effect on what beliefs we will use to set our compass for life as we travel on our soul journey.

We have explored how the beliefs that are first introduced to us form the foundation of the concepts of our physical world, our spiritual world, and our individual identity within such structures as our family, our ethnic background, and our societal beliefs. Our souls know who our tribal family will be and where we enter into the physical world in order to provide us with what we need for the continuation of our soul's journey of illumination. This placement is where we absorb the beliefs of the tribe that we have been born into, and those beliefs form our perspective of the world around us, beginning in our childhoods. We first begin at this level to learn how to manage our individual power by interacting with our environment and our fellow tribe members. The root chakra is also the chakra that strongly influences how we manage interactions with the physical world and with people.

Tribal beliefs can dictate the life course we will follow: our career path, whom we can be friends with, what is socially acceptable, whom we can marry, our spiritual beliefs, how we dress, and so on. These beliefs can not only drown out who we truly are, but they also can limit our selections from the vast plethora of choices available to us in this world. These deeply seeded beliefs influence every aspect of our lives. Our restricted judgments of what is acceptable and what is not according to our tribal standards can result in the manifestation of the thing we fear the most, should we step outside those clear restrictions: isolation and abandonment by the tribe, a sense of being alone in the world.

The strong sense of loyalty that we have to these beliefs can also be the most controlling factor in our lives, keeping us tied to the tribe throughout our lives. These early childhood beliefs can become our masters, and we become slaves to the master. Think of the story I told you about myself in the fifth decade of my life. I felt overwhelmed with a feeling of disloyalty to my mother upon letting go of the belief that I no longer wanted to be "tough." That one tribal belief that I had assimilated into how I managed my life had huge ramifications. You can understand how the beliefs introduced in our youths have the potential to be like chains throughout our lives. There is no one way to release those chains, but the spiritual journey deep within our being is essential to reaching the Truth of who we are. In the case of knowing which beliefs rule your life, ignorance is not bliss. We can end in oblivion.

Our first attempt at striving for independence from tribal control is when we decide we want more autonomy. It is then that we begin to display what psychologists call oppositional behavior. Some psychologists even label this stage in our development the first adolescence, which most of us know as the terrible twos. Our second attempt at becoming individuals is during adolescence, the classic acting-out behavior. Most of us follow this natural maturation process, which really is a necessary developmental stage on our way to our individual identities. We begin to strike out on our own, distancing ourselves from our tribal identity, which broadens from our immediate family and familiar surroundings. Unfortunately for most of us, we simply swapped old limitations for new ones, no matter how foolish they may have made us look or act in ridding ourselves of the old. Think of some of the things you wore or how you styled your hair during your teen years. If you are like me, you shrink from pictures of yourself during that period. Imagine what must have been going on internally. I cringe just thinking about my own experience.

What we are unaware of is that we have simply moved into the illusion of freedom that we believed our new tribe would afford us. The new tribal beliefs deceive us into believing that we now belong to something bigger than ourselves, the new tribe, if you will, when in reality we are likewise bound by the laws and traditions of the new tribe. This journey may provide a temporary sense of being connected to self but is usually short-lived and disappointing. However, it is a component of the path of *neti, neti* that is necessary to find the Truth of who we are.

This adopting of new tribes and tribal beliefs will continue through most of our lives. We may pass through the career tribe and the beliefs we picked up on our educational journey to reach our goals: the devoted partner; our partners' ideals of a romantic relationship; the parent tribe if we have children; the standards of current child rearing; and so on. Each journey provides us with the experience of what others believe. We take those elements and incorporate them into our belief systems.

After experimenting with a new rebellious self, though, many of us slowly slide back into many of the core tribal beliefs of our childhoods. For most of us this is an unconscious process. Some of us choose specific original beliefs, fully embrace them, and call them our own, not knowing they are not original. We may become aware that we have indeed brought some of our unwanted tribal baggage along when suddenly we realize it and respond with, "Oh my God, I sound just like my mother (or father, etc.). How could this be happening? I swore to myself I would never ever say (or do) this!"

Some of us may be alert enough to realize what has happened to us. We do indeed sound like our parents despite our best efforts. My experience is that most of us take this awareness of carrying some tribal baggage as an interesting observation and then proceed on our unconscious way, dragging that baggage with us. We do not take the opportunity to delve into what other tribal beliefs we might be carrying, that we are obviously unaware of. If you are like me, you continue without acknowledging that deep call within, even though you intuitively know your present life is not your true path or calling and that the life you should be living is quite different from the one you are living. Life seems to *happen* to us. We ride the waves as best we can. Some waves are gentle and soothing, some challenging and thrilling, some tumultuous and disturbing. Then, of course, there are the tsunamis, which are life altering.

Whatever the configuration of the call from our soul, whether subtle or explosive, we intuitively know we are still yearning for something that most of us cannot even describe, but we know it is "there." When the desire to listen to the call becomes so strong it silences the constant chatter of "shoulds" in our minds, we begin to expand our exploration of why we do the things we do and what we truly value. Doing so is commonly a fairly tumultuous time in our lives, not only for us but also for those around us. We find ourselves questioning the validity of the tribal beliefs on which we have been basing our life choices.

Universal Beliefs

As we open ourselves to the guidance of our souls, we start to make choices based on new values, consciously or unconsciously. We energetically draw toward us the information and the teachers that will assist us on the journey of our souls — not just formal teachers but individuals we encounter in our daily lives, including those master teachers, the *noble adversaries*. Books with spiritual themes, movies with symbolic messages of being true to self, and brochures offering classes that foster self-growth — information in any format we need to move forward on the journey — flow into our lives to help us. Spiritual and mystical teachings may start to resonate deeply within our beings, and we can no longer deny that we are becoming more aligned to the Truth of who we are.

When we chose to take this path seriously, finally knowing that it really is not optional in finding true peace within, things begin to move along at a much swifter pace. It is difficult to determine whether we are really making progress on the journey. One way that I have found helpful is the amount of joy I experience when I become aware of someone else receiving a blessing or boon. This is an indication that I am connected to something that is not centered in my ego.

GOING WITHIN: Take this opportunity to explore your beliefs again. This time, focus on the tribal beliefs you received in your childhood. Think deeply about which core beliefs you have carried with you from your original tribe. Chose a few to reflect on. Do not choose any beliefs previously chosen. Close your eyes, travel your well-worn path to your place of stillness, and try to discover the impact the beliefs you chose are having on your life today, positive or negative. Write in your journal about your thoughts and feelings. Again, humbly ask that Divine grace reveal the truth about the beliefs that continue to influence your life. Ask yourself whether they still serve your soul and whether you want to keep them as they are, alter them slightly, or release them. As in previous reflections, create a ritual to release, respectfully and lovingly, what is no longer serving your soul.

≈

We Are All One

As I noted previously, when we change our belief system, even just one belief, our thoughts and actions change, which inevitably sets off a chain reaction. Our surroundings shift to align with the energy of the change and, consequently, the way we interact with our surroundings shifts dramatically. You can expect your interactions with others to shift to align with your new energy pattern. Be patient with yourself and others as you move forward. You know the changes you have made in your belief system and that you committed to making them after serious contemplation. Yet those around you will continue to interact with the you they were accustomed to. I have found there is a definite lag time for those around me in realizing that I am not reacting to things in the same way. I encourage you not to be discouraged and go back to your old ways or become angry at the inability of others to note how much you have changed.

Moving from your immediate connection to your extended family and friends and into your community in today's technological times can involve a hugely larger area than your previous circle of interactions. You may have served your community before, in the belief that you wanted to make a difference in the world around you. When your beliefs shift to a much more expansive view of what the world around you means, you become aware of the significance of all your thoughts, words, and deeds because they are now based in the field of vibrational energy that is universal. Our beliefs and actions are then based on the principle that we are all *One*. When we serve our communities, we are really serving ourselves.

The words of Christ, "The Father and I are One" and "Do unto others as you would have them do unto you," are rooted in the mystical law that we are all One. I have found another of Christ's teachings helpful in releasing me from the bondage of the illusion that we are not interconnected. It is, "Know the Truth and the Truth will set you free," the Truth being that we are One with our Creator. Serve your community, however you define it, from the place of your new awareness of the interconnectedness of all life, seeing Spirit in all things. Serve, remaining congruent with the wisdom of your soul in all your actions. Serve without attachment to the outcome of your actions, knowing that the purity of your heart will shine through and that the highest outcome will be determined by a consciousness beyond your understanding.

The quotations at the beginning of this chapter refer to the Oneness of the universe. You can see that we are back where we started with the crown chakra's message of Oneness in chapter two. The quote from the Emerald Tablet tells us that the energy that is within one part of creation is the same as what is within all other aspects of creation. We are made from the Oneness of the universe. What we do affects all other things in the universe because of that connectedness. Saint Francis of Assisi wrote, "What we are looking for is what is looking." Rabbi Lawrence Kushner tells us that when we hold up our hands before our eyes, we are looking at the hands of God. In chapter two I have described different ways to attempt to comprehend the inexplicable aspect of the Oneness of creation. You might want to review them now that you have traveled this far in your journey.

The awareness that we are all One brings us to the challenge of viewing the beliefs of other tribes as being based on the same universal laws and principles as ours. Granted, we dress drastically different than, for example, the Masai tribes in Kenya and Tanzania, but many of their beliefs are similar to ours, even though they have retained their tribal lifestyle in the bush, where their ancestors have lived for thousands of years. I had the fortunate experience of being at one of their villages in Kenya while on a safari. During my travels I spoke with one of the tribesmen. He was about thirty years old. At that time I was still working as a clinical nurse specialist in the HIV/AIDS field and was well aware of the devastating effect that pandemic was having throughout Africa. I respectively broached the subject with this gentle man, who began a sophisticated conversation with me. We discussed the aspect of access to HIV/AIDS prevention and care in his isolated area of the country.

He immediately told me of a clinic that was about a two-day walk from his village, where everyone had access to condoms and HIV care. He said that not many people went there, because they were fearful of being identified as having AIDS, even if they were at the clinic simply for condoms. This is the *exact* same conversation I had been having with people in my practice on the other side of the globe for years — the same belief, minus the two-day walk. Though ours was not a deep conversation on spiritual or family beliefs, you can plainly see that the fears of being identified were the same. I am sure that had the tribesman had time to talk longer with me, we would have had other conversations and found we had similar beliefs.

This is a simple example of how deep within our being is the human thread that connects us all. It speaks to the need of accepting others as part of the human tribe and then stretching our beliefs to include all species and tribes, from organisms to plants to animals, from the microcosm to the macrocosm, and on to infinity. This belief of Oneness is again present in other words of Christ: "Whatever you did for one of the least of these brothers and sisters of mine, you did for me." We will never have peace in our world until we live according to such principles. We are they and they are us. We are indeed a family.

Even quantum physics reveals a connectedness to the universe that we are not thoroughly aware of. It is reflected in the quotation at the beginning of this chapter by Erwin Schrodinger. He was an Austrian physicist and theoretical biologist. He was awarded the Nobel Prize in physics in 1933 and was a personal friend of Albert Einstein. He also received the honor of having a crater on the moon named after him. He is considered one of the fathers of quantum physics.

Ervin Laszlo, a doctor of the philosophy of science, system theorist, and author, has discussed *quanta* as follows:

"Among 'quanta,' the smallest discernible units of the physical world, a direct form of 'information-transmission' has come to light, known as 'entanglement.' In their pristine state — in the absence of measurements or another form of interaction — quanta are 'entangle' with each other. Every quantum in the world is entangled with every other quantum. The physical universe is connected beyond the ordinary limits of space and time. In the terminology of the renowned physicist David Bohm, all things throughout the world are connected by *in-formation*—all things 'in-form' each other..."

"Could these 'nonlocal' entanglements persist over time? Evidence indicates that they do. But if so, then the information present in the world must be encoded somehow in the universe. The simplest scientific explanation is that it is encoded in a universal field."

"It is this Akashic (Sanskrit for space) in-formation field that I have been accessing since I was a child. It is the same field that artist, poets, prophets, and scientists access in their moments of creativity, enlightenment, and inspiration. It is the same field that we all access when we experience profound awe, elation, empathy, and joy. And that we access when we feel the love that binds all things in heaven and on earth."

GOING WITHIN: These beliefs of Oneness are difficult to grasp. As you ponder these concepts of the connectedness of the universe that have come from such varied sources, it should give you pause to question your tribal beliefs of "them versus us" (if you have them). Do those concepts affect your current beliefs and consequently your thoughts and actions? Take the opposite approach as well: Reflect on the concept that we are *not One.* How do you explain the mystical experiences recounted by the sages through the ages that tell us the same principles and that are backed by scientific research? Take time now to reflect on the concepts, and write about what you discover.

Now think about why you believe what you do regarding the concept of Oneness and where the beliefs come from, remembering that self-knowledge is essential to your spiritual growth. Has either side of the concept of Oneness opened your mind to a different way of being present in your world? Be sure to write your thoughts in your journal. I guarantee they will change as time goes on and it will be interesting to read about the expansion of your awareness and consciousness. If this simple reflection has shifted your belief even slightly, that shift will certainly have an impact on how you navigate the course of your days, as well as the thoughts and beliefs you carry within your soul.

~

Choosing the Ripples We Make

My experience is that the more I perceive and interact with my surroundings, conscious of being part of the Oneness of life, the more my world becomes expansive and unlimited. As a result, I hold myself to a much higher standard in my daily thoughts, words, and actions. We are all on a never-ending expansion of awareness. As our awareness expands, so does our understanding, to which we need to hold ourselves accountable. We will need to live at a higher level of consciousness, one that includes an awareness that what we think, say, and do affects everything because of the energetic vibrational frequencies that are set in motion. These concepts can deepen our belief that we are indeed One with all that is, even if we choose to see the belief on a purely physical plane. My belief is grounded in the spiritual knowing that we are all part of the Oneness of God.

Think of yourself as being like a pebble dropped into a still pond, creating ripples that reach to the end of that pond, affecting all that is in and on the pond. The time to choose whether to be in the pond has long past. You are here. The choice now is deciding what effect you want your presence here to have. The choice has always been up to you, but maybe you are just awakening to that realization. I encourage you to choose consciously the effect you will have on the whole, otherwise you will make an unconscious choice. However, have no doubt whatsoever, you *will* affect the whole. When you do not like what you see in the pond, do as Mahatma Gandhi told us, "Become the change you want to see in the world." Based on the principle of the Oneness of creation exposed throughout this book, the change you make will undoubtedly affect the whole of creation.

We realize that by opening ourselves to the blessings we have received, we fortify our souls with the stamina to continue onward, toward union with the Divine in preparation for receiving complete illumination. This process is undoubtedly accelerated when we ask for Divine grace to light our way and reveal to us the many Truths that will illuminate the journey of our souls. Powered by compassion and unconditional love, we will see others as God's creations. No longer will they be our competitors in the world of the illusion of duality. As we become conscious that our "tribe" has expanded to include all creation, humanity as well as all creatures and all life forms, we will live in the awareness that what we do to one, we do to all. We then begin to realize that we are a part of creation, that our presence is just as important as that of "the other," and that the other's presence is just as important as ours. We truly are "all in this together," like the title of one of the songs on Carole King's album, *Wrap Around Joy*:

> *We are all in this together*
> *And maybe we'll see that one day*
> *When we conquer our fear together*
> *When we finally find a way.*

CHAPTER 9

EXPLORING DIFFERENT CHAKRA CONFIGURATIONS

A T THE BEGINNING OF THIS BOOK I mentioned that I would be focusing on the seven most commonly referred to chakras. Although some authors have referred to other chakras, my inspiration was based on the seven-chakra system, and therefore I continue to use that system in presenting the configurations of those seven chakras. These configurations will add to your understanding of how those energy centers interact in ways that might help you in your journey of enlightenment.

You are already aware that your three upper chakras are primarily involved with managing your inner world. Your three lower chakras operate similarly with your exterior world, and your heart chakra serves as your spiritual birthplace. In the configuration that I have presented, top down versus bottom up, the heart chakra serves as the sacred place where you give birth to the wisdom that has been revealed to you. When going within in your three upper chakras to contemplate and reflect on new concepts, this wisdom flows into your lower chakras, allowing that wisdom to influence your self-esteem and how you "show up" in the exterior world through the energy of the solar plexus chakra. The wisdom influences how you interact one-on-one with others, how you open yourself to creative inspiration, and how you experience the exterior world with your senses through the energy of the sacral chakra. Lastly, this wisdom influences your ability to become grounded and feel safe in your external world. Consequently, this new awareness will have a significant effect on how you view the world because of the illumination of your tribal beliefs. This new awareness will be projected into the exterior world through the energy of the root chakra.

THE PARTNERING OF CHAKRAS

When a being becomes enlightened, experiencing alignment with universal consciousness in the crown chakra, he or she can drop his or her body and leave the earthly plane or choose to return to the physical realm, serving humanity as a teacher. When such beings choose to return to the realm of space and time, the place of *maya*, or illusion, they are no longer affected by the illusion of duality that is formed in the egoic mind, as they are able to remain in the consciousness of enlightenment. They have obtained *moksha*, a Sanskrit word meaning release or liberation, from duality. Let us look at how the world would be viewed from that illuminated perception of these chakras patterns.

We look at each chakra and partner it with another chakra in terms of their similarities, with the exception of the heart chakra. I view the heart chakra as being between the upper and lower energy centers, serving as a womb, if you will, radiating the wisdom of the higher, illuminated chakras. We can view these energy centers from a different perspective when they are partnered according to their similarities.

Keep in mind that I am describing the energy of the chakras after they have been illuminated. The crown and the root chakras together share a similarity you are already familiar with, the theme of Oneness. The Oneness of universal, or cosmic consciousness, which occurs in the crown chakra, and the Oneness of creation in the root chakra have the unifying principle of Oneness. That principle reflects a universal law: What is in the One is in the Whole; the being experiences a consciousness of Oneness in the crown chakra and consequently views all creation from that awareness. The separation of tribal mentality no longer exists. In the words of Joseph Campbell, they are inert. The beliefs that separate beings are dissolved into the consciousness that everything has the presence of Spirit within it.

Moving on to the third eye and the sacral chakras, here the similarities are of duality. The illusion of separation that is created by our minds is removed, allowing the being to see Spirit in all things in the world around them. The awareness of that Oneness flows into all one-on-one relationships in the sacral energy center. The enlightened being no longer views the other as a separate being: Spirit resides within each being as One. They are One.

The last set comprises the throat and the solar plexus chakras, the similarity being choice. The enlightened being now has the awareness that choices are no longer based on a separate will — my will — but from a place of Divine will in the throat energy center. The illuminated solar plexus chakra transforms the choice of identification of self-esteem with the Truth of who we are, One with Spirit, in the interior world instead of identification with the values of the exterior world.

Heart Center Giving Spiritual Birth

Interior World Chakra		Exterior World Chakra
Crown Oneness of consciousness	→	**Root** Oneness of creation
Third Eye Liberation from duality	→	**Sacral** 1-1 relationship are now in Oneness
Throat Choice of Your will not my will	→	**Solar Plexus** Self-esteem based God not ego

I find it helpful to view the chakras in this configuration because it gives me insight into the significant difference of how to interact with the external world from a place of higher consciousness, instead of allowing the animal nature of the lower chakras to dominate my interactions with my exterior world. Striving toward this consciousness of Oneness changes every aspect of how I interact with my life.

The Three Lower Chakras

Our physical bodies are vehicles for experiencing the Divine in the realm of space and time, the world of manifested form and duality. Our soul temporarily dwells within this vehicle as it continues on its journey of illumination. Enlightened beings are able to embody the consciousness of compassion and unconditional love of the heart chakra in their interior world and bring that consciousness to the interactions with the lower chakras in their exterior world. Our three lower chakras, when not illuminated, are more susceptible to the vibrational frequency of our animal nature.

Most of us in the west are familiar with the three temptations presented to Christ when Christ was fasting in the desert for forty days. Campbell tells us that all three of these temptations were targeted at the three lower chakra energies, the animal nature in human experience. Buddha also experienced three temptations while sitting under the Bodhi Tree on his soul's journey of enlightenment. Those three temptations were directed at his animal nature as well, the tribal dictates of the root chakra, the desires of the sacral chakra, and the fear-based reality of the solar plexus chakra. The temptations were unsuccessful, because Christ and Buddha were enlightened beings.

When we are able to glimpse illumination in our heart chakra, the energy of our lower chakras is affected as well. This glimpse of illumination can transform our ability to recognize the Oneness of creation, affecting our perception of the exterior world. We can begin the transformational process of no longer viewing our exterior world through the view of our "not being good enough" in the solar plexus chakra, as us against them in the sacral chakra, and us against the world in the root chakra. One of the quotations from chapter two was *Tat Twam Asi,* Thou Art That, "That" representing Spirit. When we are able to view the exterior world from this higher consciousness, it shifts our perception to:

SOLAR PLEXUS CHAKRA

I am That, when I am aligned with the Divine within instead of I am not good enough.

SACRAL CHAKRA

You, the other person, is That, when I am aligned with the Divine within instead of me against you.

ROOT CHAKRA

They, the tribe, are That when I am aligned with the Divine within instead of me against the world.

THIS POEM FROM RUMI REFLECTS THIS MESSAGE:

Soul of all souls, life of all life — you are That.
Seen and unseen, moving and unmoving — you are That.
The road that leads to the City is endless:
Go without head or feet
And you'll already be there.
What else could you be? — You are That.
—Mawlana Jalal-al-Din Rumi

THE CHAKRAS: ONE WAY
TO VIEW OUR EARTHLY LIFE

The next configuration of the seven-chakra system is based on the traditional format in which the chakras are presented: beginning at the root chakra and rising to the crown chakra. This system also contains the principle of the Kundalini energy, which lies dormant in the root chakra. *Kundalini* is a Sanskrit word that translates as "coiled up," and the Kundalini is depicted as coiled energy in the form of a serpent contained in the root chakra. Various spiritual practices, such as Kundalini yoga, self-inquiry meditation, and breathing practices are designed to "awaken" this serpent so the dormant energy may rise up through each chakra alongside the spine. As this energy awakens each chakra, the awakening of higher consciousness occurs, with the ultimate enlightened experience occurring in the crown chakra, which is the experience of Oneness with creation, the key word being *experience*. Sri Ramana Maharshi described this Kundalini energy as the force that all are created with, as well as the cosmic consciousness that it contains. However, this cosmic consciousness is hidden by the illusions that the mind creates when we are in the realm of time, space, and form. When a person's cosmic consciousness has been experienced, the term *Nirvana* is used by some traditions to describe the experience of Oneness.

Joseph Campbell beautifully and knowledgeably describes the effects Kundalini energy has on each chakra as it rises to its goal: the illumination of the crown chakra. He presented the chakras configured in the shape of a triangle and believed that this describes "a way to translate our earthly experience into a spiritual practice."

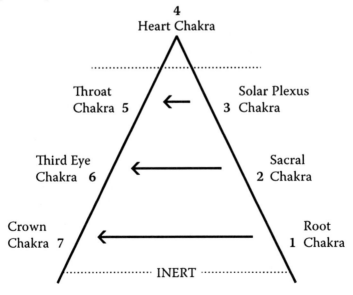

When an enlightened being experiences cosmic consciousness, he or she can choose to be released from life and drop his or her body or remain in the earthly plane. In the configuration of the chakras on the previous page, Campbell places the heart chakra at the top of the triangle to demonstrate that it is where the enlightened being chooses to have its consciousness return when the being returns to the earthly plane to be a teacher, thereby serving humanity. The enlightened being transforms the energy of the solar plexus that once focused on control in the external world and turns its energies toward the interior world to conquer illusions and attachments. The energy of the sacral chakra transforms its human love in the external world to love of the Divine in the interior world. The enlightened being chooses to return to life as a teacher (as Buddha did after enlightenment). The energy of the root chakra has become inert since the enlightened being is beyond any attachment at the earthly level. The crown chakra is fully illuminated, and consciousness is of the Oneness of all things.

THE SIGN OF INFINITY

The last configuration I suggest to you is the sign for infinity, rotated vertically to align with the seven chakras. The inspiration for this configuration came to me in the beginning stages of writing this book. In chapter one, at the beginning of my discussion of the chakra system, I shared with you that the chakras continually affect one another. They are aligned with the universal law of "What is in the One is in the Whole," just as all creation is. Keeping that in mind, you can easily see that the sign for infinity is an appropriate representation of the chakra system, whose energies do not have a beginning or an end.

Crown Chakra

Third Eye Chakra

Throat Chakra

Heart Chakra

Solar Plexus Chakra

Sacral Chakra

Root Chakra

Note that as in the other configurations, the heart chakra plays a central role in the transformative process of illuminating the animal-like nature of the lower chakras in this configuration as well.

CONCLUSION

CROSSING THE THRESHOLD

I HAVE LONG BEEN A FAN of Shirley MacLaine's writings. Although I do not agree with everything she writes, I have found her insights edifying. I read something of hers that seemed most appropriate on the morning after I sent the bulk of this book to my editor. I share with you what MacLaine wrote in regard to the seven chakras and her thinking that they might be connected to the Revelation by St. John the Divine (not to be confused with St. John of the Cross, about whom I have previously written). The Revelation is the last book of the New Testament in the Christian Bible. I paraphrase her words in *Sage-ing While Age-ing,* but first a little background for those of you who are not familiar with the Revelation.

Saint John the Divine was a disciple of Christ who wrote a gospel in the New Testament in addition to the Revelation: the Apocalypse, what some people refer to as the end of this world. He reports on visions of heaven and conflicts between the opposing forces of good and evil. The writings go on in great detail about how this will unfold and what to be mindful of. The writings use symbolic and allegorical language, and no one is really sure what the symbols and allegories represent.

MacLaine poses this question, "What if St. John the Divine wrote Revelations [sic] as an acknowledged blueprint for [human] consciousness?" She suggests that the seven churches, the seven candlesticks, and the seven seals that St. John refers to in the Revelation might be related to our seven chakras, and that the things St. John wrote about could be allegories for the struggle between our light and our shadow that we encounter when we face challenges. I thought this was an interesting concept. Certainly we do battle when we go within to search our souls to determine the Truth of who we are, confronting our shadow on the way to reaching for the light. The struggle between our light and our shadow may be viewed from a similar perspective. One hopes that the casualties of our inner confrontations will be our conflicting beliefs that no longer serve us, past traumas that we lose energy to by dragging them around with us, and the illusions of our egoic minds.

This inner conflict also has tones of the common stages of the hero's journey:

1. Ordinary World: The hero's normal world before the story begins.

2. Call to Adventure: The hero is presented with a problem, challenge, or adventure.

3. Refusal of the Call: The hero refuses the challenge or journey, usually because he is scared.

4. Meeting with the Mentor: The hero meets a mentor to gain advice or training for the adventure.

5. Crossing the First Threshold: The hero crosses, leaves the ordinary world, and goes into the special world.

6. Test, Allies, Enemies: The hero faces tests, meets allies, confronts enemies, and learns the rules of the special world.

7. Approach: The hero hits setbacks during tests and may need to try a new idea.

8. Ordeal: The biggest life or death crisis.

9. Reward: The hero survives death, overcomes his fear, and now earns the reward.

10. The Road Back: The hero must return to the ordinary world.

11. Resurrection Hero: Another test where the hero faces death. He has to use everything he has learned.

12. Return with Elixir: The hero returns from the journey with the "elixir" and uses it to help everyone in the ordinary world.

Let us see how our soul's journey matches up with the hero's journey:
1. Ordinary World: Our exterior world.

2. Call to Adventure: The call deep within our souls that something is not right with our lives.

3. Refusal of the Call: We want to keep the status quo of our lives even though we intuitively know we are not whole. Yet we are too afraid of the unknown and the consequences that change could bring to our exterior world.

4. Meeting the Mentor: A synchronistic meeting with a spiritual teacher or the contents of a workshop or a book that serves as a mentor, giving us direction on how to answer the call of our souls.

5. Crossing the First Threshold: We leave our exterior world to go deeply within our interior world to meet our soul. We are blessed with Divine grace and guidance.

6. Tests, Allies, Enemies: We face our beliefs, fears, and ego-centered mind in our inner world. We learn how to humbly approach the Divine, our constant ally, for assistance.

7. Approach: We try to implement the wisdom we have received from the Divine but are not able to hold our center when challenged by the exterior world.

8. Ordeal: It is too late to turn around and go back to our old beliefs now that we are conscious of how they no longer serve our soul. We cannot un-ring that bell, but we are almost paralyzed with fear by what is happening to life as we once knew it.

9. Reward: We have a sense of peace and self-assuredness and are becoming confident in our new beliefs.

10. The Road Back: We come back prepared to become fully present in the exterior world.

11. Resurrection Hero: We meet a *noble adversary* who challenges the progress we have made. We are able to hold our center in compassion and unconditional love, seeing the "other" as part of the Oneness of creation.

12. Return with Elixir: We return to the external world and share the wisdom we have received with all those who are suffering as a result of not being aligned with the Truth of who they are.

≈

This sounds a lot like the journey we have begun and what lies ahead of us. William Butler Yeats, the Nobel Prize laureate for his "inspired" poetry, tells us: "The only journey worth taking is the one within our self." Are you up for the challenge? Remember, God does not call the qualified. He qualifies the called. What are you being called to do? Is it time to begin this journey for real this time? You know where your resources are when you stumble, become confused, or are frightened. Go within to the energy center of the chakra that reflects the challenge you are losing your power to, and reverently ask for Divine grace and guidance to lead you to Truth.

Thank you for joining me on this never-ending journey of discovering the Truth of who we are: one with Spirit. You can stay where you are in your soul's journey, which is exactly where you are meant to be, or you can humbly and reverently ask for Divine grace, the power that can illuminate your soul, to move you along and quicken your pace. As always, the choice is yours and no one else's.

≈

Not long ago, on the day I completed this book, during my morning meditation, I heard the words "go beyond" over and over again; I could not quiet my mind. Suddenly I remembered an extraordinary CD I had bought on my cross-country trip. Dechen Shak-Dagsay and Regula Curti combined Buddhist and Christian prayers and sang them with voices like those of angels. These amazing artists then invited Tina Turner to become part of their spiritual endeavor. Tina Turner introduces the sacred sounds with words inspired by Deepak Chopra and Rumi. I want to leave you with those most beautiful and inspiring words from that CD, *Beyond*. Here are some of the words that I feel in my heart capture the essence of this book:

"SPIRITUAL MESSAGE"

Nothing lasts forever, no one lives forever, the flower that fades and dies, the winter passes, and spring comes, embrace the cycle of life, that is the greatest love.

GO BEYOND FEAR
Beyond fear takes you into the place where love grows, when you refuse to follow the impulses of fear, anger, and revenge.

BEYOND MEANS TO FEEL YOURSELF
We all need a repeated discipline, a genuine training to let go of our old habits of mind and to find and sustain a new way of seeing.

GO BEYOND THE RIGHTS AND THE WRONGS
Prayer clears the head and brings back peace to the soul.

GO BEYOND TO FEEL THE O-n-e-ness OF THE UNITY
We are all the same, all the same, looking to find our way back to the source, to the One, to the only One.

GO BEYOND REVENGE
The greatest moment in our lives is when we allow us to teach each other.

TAKE THE JOURNEY INSIDE OF YOU
To become quiet to hear the beyond. To become patient to receive the beyond. To become open to invite the beyond and be grateful to allow the beyond. Be in the present moment to live in the beyond.

WHAT DOES LOVE HAVE TO DO WITH IT
LOVE grows when you trust. When you trust, LOVE heals and renews. LOVE inspires and empowers us to do great things and makes us a better person to love. LOVE makes us feel safe and brings us closer to GOD.

Beyond right and wrong, there is a field.
I'll meet you there.
Mawlana Jalal-al-Din Rumi

APPENDIX I

THIS IS ONE OF THE PRAYERS I SAY BEFORE MEDITATION:

Lord, I humbly ask for Your Divine grace to illuminate my consciousness with Oneness.

Lord, I humbly ask for Your Divine grace to illuminate my mind so it may be beyond illusion, judgment, and opinionating and aligned with You.

Lord, I humbly ask for Your Divine grace to illuminate all my choices in thoughts, words, and deeds so my will is aligned with Your will.

Lord, I humbly ask for Your Divine grace to illuminate my heart so it is aligned with the sacredness of Divinity.

Lord, I humbly ask for Your Divine grace to illuminate my sense of self with the Truth of who I am at the time of my making.

Lord, I humbly ask for Your Divine grace to illuminate my senses so I may experience You more thoroughly, my creativity so I may receive Your Divine inspiration, and my ability to see You in each being I interact with this day.

Lord, I humbly ask for Your Divine grace to illuminate the fears and beliefs that no longer serve my soul and my ability to see the face of Divinity in all life forms, knowing what is in the One is in the Whole.

APPENDIX II

THE FOLLOWING are different meditation practices I have used throughout the years. I have found it is most helpful to meditate in the same place and at the same time of day whenever possible. This consistent practice prepares our bodies and our minds for meditation in a habitual manner.

Find a time and place to meditate where you will have the least distraction. It can be helpful to meditate in a sitting position on the floor with a small pillow or rolled towel under your coccyx. The pillow will raise your hips slightly to relieve the pressure on your hip joints. I light a candle, smudge, and then pray before I begin to meditate.

Eckhart Tolle teaches that you cannot concentrate on your breath and have a thought at the same time. Many people focus on their breath in a rhythmic pattern as a way to go beyond the mind and thoughts into the stillness of the present, the Now.

Quiet your mind, take a few calming breaths, and become centered. Gently close your eyes and begin your breathing. When you become aware that you are thinking, simply go back to your rhythmic breathing pattern without judgment or resistance.

Repeating a mantra, a word, group of words, or sound can help still the mind. A mantra that is familiar in the yogic tradition is "so hum." This is the sound that the breath makes, but it also represents a contemplative practice of repeating two words: *so*, meaning "I am," and *hum*, meaning "that," or all that is. Repeat "so" on the in breath and "hum" on the out breath. Follow the instructions regarding quieting your mind, take a few calming breaths, and begin repeating the mantra.

Some of you may be familiar with the words "Be still and know that I am God." Many people use them as a meditation. Quiet your mind, as before, taking a few deep breaths, and become centered. Begin with the full prayer, and then remove words as follows:

MEDITATIVE PRACTICE
Be still and know that I am God
Be still and know that I am
Be still and know
Be still
Be

Take long periods of contemplation after each line before you proceed to the next line. You may repeat this over and over. Listen for the silence in the stillness.

James Finley, whom I write about in this book, shares this meditative practice. The words are meant to evoke deep peace and unconditional love within. Quiet your mind, take a few breaths, and become centered. Repeat the following words with each inhale and exhale. Focus on your breath and the devotion connected to the words.

MEDITATIVE PRACTICE

On the inhale: I love you. (This is God saying this to you.)

On the exhale: I love You. (This is you saying this to God.)

This is the prayer I say after my meditation: "Thank you Lord for illuminating my consciousness, my mind, my will, and my heart. Thank you for illuminating my sense of self. Thank for illuminating my senses, my creativity, and my ability to see You in each being I interact with this day. Thank you for illuminating the fears and beliefs that no longer serve my soul and for my ability to see the face of Divinity in all life forms, knowing that what is in the One is in the Whole. I am truly appreciative, thankful, and blessed."

ACKNOWLEDGMENTS

THE WRITING OF THIS BOOK has been a challenging journey for me, both inwardly and externally, in every way. Without knowing that this material was given to me for a purpose, I moved forward into the field of becoming an author with minimal skills and great trepidation. I never stopped to ask how I was to do this, as somehow I knew questioning the instruction I received to "write this" was not optional. Fortunately for me, I have been blessed with supportive family members and friends who encouraged me and who many times brought their light to remove the shadow of self-doubt that visited me regularly.

I want to begin by thanking Nancy Simmons for her review of my original manuscript and using such gentle words of encouragement, while graciously letting me know that I needed the help of a meticulous editor. She wrote a letter of introduction to her colleague, Lorraine Alexson, editor extraordinaire. Lorraine, on many occasions, took my words and positioned them in such a fashion that I was impressed with my own writing. She has been an exceptional gift and source of expertise. I will be eternally grateful.

When I approached Jim Curtan, a faculty member of Caroline Myss's CMED Institute, motivational speaker, and spiritual director, to write the foreword to my book, his response was "I would be honored." The reality is, I am honored that he would take time from his full schedule of guiding others on their spiritual journeys for me.

I could not have asked for a more supportive and loving husband than Paul for this journey. His patience, encouragement, and willingness to temporarily put our life together on the back burner allowed me to focus on this endeavor. He was a source of strength and courage for me during many difficult challenges that appeared on this passage.

There is no way I can thank enough my soul companion, Tinna Savini. She lifted me up through many difficult times. Her belief in me and in the message of this book never wavered. She was always there to offer selfless encouragement and suggestions. Her talent and vision brought beauty and clarity to many concepts I struggled to frame in words.

I profoundly thank the circle of family and friends who gave freely of their time to read the manuscript at various stages of its development. My daughter Jessica Hudop, a busy mom and entrepreneur, offered her insight and encouragement along the way. Nadine Clegern, Resa Ferreira, Kerry Green, Gail Ide, Ann Messecar, and John von Lonkhuyzen offered their heartfelt suggestions and encouragement, for which I am most grateful.

Last, and by no means least, I thank God for the gift of this book, mystically given to me on that cold, dark morning in March. I knew my world was rocked in that instant, but I could never have foreseen the changes it would make in my soul and, consequently, in my life. I will be eternally awestruck by the mystery of Divine grace, the power that continues to illuminate my soul.

Bibliography

Anonymous. *The Cloud of Unknowing, trans. William Johnston.* New York: Image Book, 1973.

Bourgeault, Cynthia. *The Wisdom Way of Knowing.* San Francisco, Calif.: Josey-Bass, 2003.

Braden, Gregg. *The DiViNE MATRIX.* Carlsbad, Calif.: Hay House, 2007.

Campbell, Joseph. *Reflections on the Art of Living: A Joseph Campbell Companion,* edited by Diane Osborn. New York: Harper Collins Publishers 1991

Campbell, Joseph. *The Hero with a Thousand Faces.* Princeton, N.J.: Princeton University Press, 1968.

Finley, James. *Merton's Palace of Nowhere.* Notre Dame, Ind.: Ave Maria Press, 2003.

Finley, James. *Thomas Merton's Palace of Nowhere.* Audio CD, 2005.

Haisch, Bernard. The *God Theory: Universes, Zero-Point Fields, and What's Behind It All*. San Francisco, Calif.: Red Wheel/Weiser, LLC, 2006.

Jung, C. G., et al. *Man and His Symbols*. Garden City, N.Y.: Doubleday, 1964.

Ladinsky, Daniel. *I Heard God Laughing: Poems of Hope and Joy, Renderings by Hafiz*. New York: Penguin Books, 2006.

McGinn. Bernard. *The Mystical Thought of Meister Eckhart: The Man from Whom God Hid Nothing*. New York: A Herder and Herder Book, 2001.

Myss, Caroline. *Anatomy of the Spirit*. New York: Random House, 1997.

Newberg, Andrew, M.D., and Mark Robert Waldman. *How God Changes Your Brain*. New York: Ballantine Books, 2009.

St. Teresa of Avila. *The Interior Castle*, trans. Mirabai Starr. New York: Riverhead Books, 2003.

Tolle, Eckhart. *The Power of Now: A Guide To Spiritual Enlightenment*. Novato, Calif.: New World Library and Vancouver, B.C., Canada: Namaste Publishing, 1999.

Turner, Tina., Dechen, Shak-Dagsay., Curti, Regula. *Beyond* CD, New Earth Records, 2010.

Vaughan-Lee, Llewellyn. *Love is a Fire: The Sufi's Mystical Journey Home*. Point Reyes Station, Calif.: The Golden Sufi Center, 2011.

Williamson, Marianne. *Return To Love*. New York: Harper One, 1992.

Index

ABOUT THE AUTHOR

AFTER DECADES of caring for the physical body of her patients as a Registered Nurse (RN) and in the HIV/AIDS arena as an AIDS Certified Registered Nurse (ACRN), Fredericka retired from her distinguished nursing career to devote more of her energy and skill to serving others in helping them see and heal their spiritual body. Open to finding and supporting Spirit in whatever form it may present itself, she has studied Buddhism, Hinduism and the spiritual traditions of native peoples of America. She has traveled to many sacred sites in Israel, Spain, and Egypt and has studied in India.

Working within the Sathya Sai Baba Organization, Close's writing experience and teaching skills were employed when she taught the "Education in Human Values" course to children, making a valuable contribution to the educational materials in the United States teacher-training curriculum. She went on to become the president of a Sathya Sai Baba Center and traveled to India many times as part of her spiritual quest of knowledge of the true Self.

She experienced a weeklong desert intensive with a Yaqui Shaman and has had the honor of hosting monthly Lakota sacred sweat lodge ceremonies on the land where she lives with her husband. It is from a deep awareness of the mystical truth, "All is One", that she furthered her studies with those working from interfaith templates, including James Finley, clinical psychologist and former Trappist monk. For over nine years, Close has studied with Caroline Myss, five times New York Times bestselling author and internationally renowned teacher of human consciousness and mysticism and has received her Sacred Contracts Certification from Caroline Myss's Institute (CMED).

FOR FURTHER INFORMATION,
PLEASE CONTACT FREDERICKA AT:

SACRED CONTRACTS CONSULTING
860-872-2911
www.sacredcontractsconsulting.com
close@sacredcontractsconsulting.com

CPSIA information can be obtained at www.ICGtesting.com
Printed in the USA
BVOW04*0509310713

326764BV00001B/1/P